100

2nd Edition

THINGS TO DO IN
SAN FRANCISCO
BEFORE YOU
DIE

100

2nd Edition

THINGS TO DO IN
SAN FRANCISCO
BEFORE YOU
DIE

• •

KIMBERLEY LOVATO
AND JILL K. ROBINSON

REEDY PRESS

Library of Congress Control Number: 2018945633

ISBN: 9781681061658

Design by Jill Halpin

Printed in the United States of America
18 19 20 21 22   5 4 3 2 1

Please note that websites, phone numbers, addresses, and company names are subject to change or cancellation. We did our best to relay the most accurate information available, but due to circumstances beyond our control, please do not hold us liable for misinformation. When exploring new destinations, please do your homework before you go.

DEDICATION

We dedicate this book to you, the curious travelers and proud San Francisco residents eager to dive deeper into this wacky and wonderful city that delivers well more than one hundred things to see and do. May this book be merely a spark that ignites your love affair with San Francisco.

CONTENTS

• •

Culture and History

• •

INTRODUCTION

How do you take a city like San Francisco and come up with only one hundred things to do? It wasn't easy, and we have a confession to make: there are actually more than one hundred addresses between these pages, and we've barely scratched the surface of all there is to see and do. We chose some "musts" for first-timers, and we've added many of our personal favorites, too. But what we really hope is that you use *100 Things to Do in San Francisco Before You Die* as a primer for tracking down what you love about San Francisco and that you return again and again to discover a new slant on this ever-transforming city.

Inside you'll find some of the best attractions, famous foods, and a few little-known must-sees for those of you who want to dig deeper into the city. You'll belly up to some of San Francisco's hippest hotel bars, eat egg tarts in Chinatown, and learn what exactly a Mission-style burrito is and where to find one. We'll clue you in on late-night dining and Dungeness crab, and we'll guide you to a world-renowned tequila bar tucked in the back of a family restaurant. Our museums are dedicated to matchless art and hands-on fun, and there's even one that hosts a cocktail party every Thursday night. You'll find out where to shop for tie-dye, browse for local and public art, follow in the footsteps of Sam Spade, and dive into the history of the Barbary Coast and the Beat Generation.

• •

San Francisco's got a musical soul, and we'll guide you to legendary venues, intimate clubs, a raucous cabaret, and free music festivals. For those who prefer a little physical exertion, you've come to the right place. Whether you climb up one of San Francisco's stairways or hills, take a guided walking tour, do yoga on a labyrinth, hike along the coastal bluffs and beaches, or get out on beautiful San Francisco Bay, calorie burning while sightseeing doesn't get better than right here in San Francisco. Of course, no book on San Francisco would be true to itself without mentioning our beloved landmarks: cable cars, the Golden Gate Bridge, Lombard Street, Coit Tower, Fisherman's Wharf, Golden Gate Park, the Presidio, and the Ferry Building. Yep, *100 Things to Do in San Francisco Before You Die* includes these, too, along with loads of information on how best to experience them.

And who are we? We are local travel journalists, adventurers, eaters and drinkers, mothers, and open-minded lovers of this great city. We have also been called the Den Mothers of Fun. It's a title we wear proudly and one we try to live up to every day. Combined, we've visited just about every corner of the world, and we couldn't imagine calling anywhere else home. We hope our wanderlust and our love of our hometown is apparent within the pages of *100 Things to Do in San Francisco Before You Die* and that it encourages you to get out and explore, whether it's your first time here or it's your own backyard. Thank you for reading, and enjoy your adventures.

—Kimberley and Jill

• •

FUN FACTS

Did you know...

1. The Japanese Tea Garden was the first place in the U.S.A. to serve sweet fortune cookies as we now know them. They were brought to San Francisco in the late 1800s by the garden's landscaper, Makoto Hagiwara.
2. Before it was renamed San Francisco, our small city by the bay was called Yerba Buena, which means "good herb" in Spanish.
3. San Francisco's Cow Hollow neighborhood got its name from the thirty-eight dairy farms that were in the area in the late nineteenth century.
4. The original United Nations Charter was signed in San Francisco at the War Memorial and Performing Arts Center on June 26, 1945.
5. The paint color used to give the Golden Gate Bridge its hue is called International Orange.
6. The building that houses the Legion of Honor Museum is a replica of the Palais de la Légion d'Honneur in Paris, also a museum.
7. San Francisco's fog has a name: Karl. Karl the Fog has a great sense of humor, along with his own Facebook,

Instagram, and Twitter accounts.

8. The model for the bear on the California state flag lived in Golden Gate Park for twenty-two years. His name was Monarch, he weighed 1,100 pounds, and he was one of the last wild grizzly bears in the state, brought to a zoo in the park in 1889.

9. San Francisco was part of Mexico until the Mexican-American War in 1848.

10. Beloved *San Francisco Chronicle* columnist Herb Caen (1916–1997) said, "One day if I do go to heaven, I'm going to do what every San Franciscan does who goes to heaven. I'll look around and say, 'It ain't bad, but it ain't San Francisco.'"

11. Lombard Street gets all the twisty love, but some say Vermont Street is actually curvier.

12. Contrary to popular belief, Mark Twain never uttered the phrase, "The coldest winter I ever spent was a summer in San Francisco." However, summers are notoriously chilly, and it's pretty much sweater weather year-round.

13. The stunning Palace of Fine Arts, built for the Panama–Pacific International Exposition in 1915, was meant to be temporary. It was saved from demolition by the Palace Preservation League and rebuilt with more permanent materials in the 1960s.

14. San Francisco has a resident flock of wild parrots.

15. In San Francisco, street names are stamped on sidewalk corners, a practice that is believed to have started after the 1906 earthquake and fire

16. The majestic dome of San Francisco's City Hall is forty-two feet taller than that of the nation's capitol.

17. On September 17, 1859, the United States was unofficially "ruled" by Joshua A. Norton, an eccentric San Franciscan who declared himself "Emperor of the United States." The local paper at the time, the *San Francisco Bulletin*, printed the decree, and Emperor Norton became a cherished local celebrity and city mascot.

18. Despite being linked to Hawaii and the South Pacific, the mai tai was allegedly invented in Emeryville, just across the Bay Bridge from San Francisco, by Victor Bergeron, the original Trader Vic.

19. Don't be alarmed if on Tuesday at noon you hear a siren bellow across the city. It's a test of San Francisco's Outdoor Warning System and sounds for 15 seconds. In an actual emergency it will cycle repeatedly for five minutes.

20. San Francisco has its own flag depicting a rising Phoenix, often assumed to be a symbol of the city's recovery from the 1906 earthquake. However the flag predates that event by a few years, and was officially adopted as the city's banner in 1940.

· ·

FOOD AND DRINK

SQUEEZE
FARM FRESH PRODUCE
AT THE FERRY BUILDING

Before the Golden Gate and Bay Bridges were built in the 1930s, boats brought commuters into the city's main port of entry, the Ferry Building. The city landmark is still a hub for waterborne transport, but most now know it as a beloved food hall filled with grocers, food shops, restaurants, and a popular thrice-weekly California certified farmers market, operated by the Center for Urban Education about Sustainable Agriculture (CUESA), that bulges with produce and goods brought in from California farmers year-round, rain or shine, on Tuesday, Thursday, and Saturday.

Embarcadero at Market St.
(415) 983-8030
ferrybuildingmarketplace.com

FUN FACT
CUESA is a nonprofit organization dedicated to cultivating a sustainable food system through the operation of farmers markets and educational programs.

TO MARKET, TO MARKET

Alemany
The oldest farmers market in California, founded in 1943.
Saturdays
100 Alemany Blvd.
(415) 647-9423

Clement Street
Small neighborhood market in the city's "other" Chinatown.
Sundays
200 Clement St. between 2nd and 4th Aves.
(415) 472-6100
agriculturalinstitute.org

Mission Community
Evening market with food, music, after-school activities,
and cultural programming.
Thursdays
Mission St. at 22nd St.
missioncommunitymarket.org

Heart of the City
Independent, farmer-operated market since 1981.
United Nations Plaza
(415) 558-9455
hotcfarmersmarket.org

BIB UP FOR A BOWL OF CIOPINNO
AT TADICH GRILL

The catchy TV commercial jingle that aired for three decades got it all wrong. The seafood stew known as cioppino, pronounced "chuh-pee-no," is the real San Francisco treat! The name comes from the word cuippin, meaning "little soup" in the Genovese dialect. It was used by Italian fishermen who came to San Francisco in the late 1800s and worked at Fisherman's Wharf. At the end of the day, they'd plop their leftover catch into pots and cook up their seafood stew. Fantastic interpretations abound at restaurants around the city, and each presents a mouthwatering masterpiece of tomato, garlic, onions, herbs, and wine along with clams, shrimp, mussels, local fish, Dungeness crab, and whatever pinch of secret zing lets their version of San Francisco's signature dish stand out. Make sure you have a loaf of crunchy sourdough bread at the ready to sop up the broth, and a bib to catch the splatter.

240 California St.
(415) 391-1849
tadichgrill.com

TIP
Tadich Grill doesn't take reservations, but it does serve more than twenty-two thousand bowls of cioppino each year.

SIP AN IRISH COFFEE
AT THE BUENA VISTA CAFE

Leave it to a writer and a bar owner to turn a boozy tale into the city's signature drink. It happened on November 10, 1952, when longtime columnist for the *San Francisco Chronicle* Stanton Delaplane sauntered into the Buena Vista Cafe, called the BV by locals, and told Jack Koeppler about a coffee and whiskey concoction he'd quaffed in Shannon, Ireland. Rumor has it Koeppler challenged Stanton to help him recreate the drink, and the duo stayed up all night pouring, mixing, and tasting. Koeppler even consulted a San Francisco dairy owner for advice on how to float the perfect cuff of cream on top. Today the Irish coffee at the BV is a rite of passage for visitors, and the best seat is at the bar, where water-heated goblets are lined up like obedient bar flies, and nearly two thousand Irish coffees per day are made by white-coated bartenders.

2765 Hyde St.
(415) 474-5044
thebuenavistsa.com

TIP
For the ultimate San Francisco day out, hop on (or off) the cable car at the Powell/Hyde cable car turnaround, just across the street from the BV.

SINK YOUR TEETH INTO AN EGG TART
AT GOLDEN GATE BAKERY

They're known as dan tat in Cantonese, but in San Francisco they are called egg tarts, and arguably the best are located in the heart of Chinatown at Golden Gate Bakery. Just look for the queue of people snaking up Grant Street, waiting to sink their teeth into buttery crusts filled with yolky, not-too-sweet custard. From a distance the tarts look like mini-lemon pies, but they are a traditional Chinese dessert. If you're familiar with the English custard tart, you'll notice the similarity to this Hong Kong cousin. Unlike the English version that has nutmeg sprinkled on top, these sunny yellow pastries are stand-alone spectacular, especially when pulled right from the oven, which happens to be the best way to eat them, too.

1029 Grant Ave.
(415) 781-2627
goldengatebakery.com

TIP
It's cash only and long lines, but definitely worth the wait.

GRAB A LITTLE "SUM-THING"
IN AMERICA'S OLDEST CHINATOWN

Far removed from the paper lanterns and tchotchke shops of Grant Street, Hang Ah Tea Room is a stumble-upon surprise on Pagoda Lane that claims the title of the oldest dim sum restaurant in the United States. First opened in 1920, Hang Ah served Chinatown's immigrant population looking for a taste of home. In recent decades, however, locals weren't sure when or even if the restaurant was open, thanks to a perpetually shuttered storefront. Current owner Frank Chui brought a few modern touches to the place—including a website and regular hours—when he bought it a few years ago. Every day, more and more neighbors and visitors discover the no-frills, low-ceilinged dining room as well as the ha gow (shrimp dumplings), gin cha siu bao (barbecue pork buns), chung yao ban (scallion pancakes), xiao long bao (soup dumplings), and other dim sum specialties.

1 Pagoda Place
(415) 982-5686
hangah1920.com

TIP
Hang Ah Tea Room now does take-out.

EAT CLAM CHOWDER IN A SOURDOUGH BREAD BOWL
AT FISHERMAN'S WHARF

Sourdough and clam chowder go together like San Francisco and fog. Want proof? Just beeline it to Fisherman's Wharf, where hollowed-out loaves become bowls filled to the brim with the piping hot soup. Stroll around and you'll see numerous signs declaring the "best chowder bowls in town." We don't doubt any of them.

Northern waterfront between Hyde St. and the Embarcadero

FUN FACT
The area known today as Fisherman's Wharf started a few blocks away at Francisco and Powell Streets, where it was called Meiggs Wharf, named for its creator, sawmill owner and lumber dealer Henry Meiggs.

TRY THESE SAVORY BOWLS

Scoma's
Four types of clams and views of actual fishermen.
1965 Al Scoma Way
(415) 771-4383
scomas.com

Alioto's
Sicilian recipes since 1925, including
Nonna's Famous Clam Chowder.
8 Fisherman's Wharf
(415) 673-0183
aliotos.com

Fog Harbor Fish House
They claim the best chowder in the city.
Pier 39, #A202
(415) 421-2442
fogharbor.com

Blue Mermaid
New England, Manhattan, and crab chowder, oh my.
471 Jefferson St.
(415) 771-2222
argonauthotel.com

FOOD TRUCK HOP
AT THE PRESIDIO PICNIC

When founder Matt Cohen launched his first pop-up gathering of food trucks, called Off the Grid, in 2010, little did he know he was birthing a beloved feeding phenomenon that would grow to more than forty-five weekly locations around the Bay Area, including this family-friendly shindig inside the historic Presidio of San Francisco. Held every Sunday between mid-March and October, the Presidio Picnic by Off the Grid and Presidio Trust unwinds on the sloping green grass of the Main Post and is flanked by a variety of San Francisco's best food trucks. Come hungry and try anything from doughnuts to empanadas, ice cream to fresh squeezed lemonade, tacos to dumplings, and much more. You'll also find games, live DJ music, morning yoga classes, and even arts and crafts for kids.

210 Lincoln Blvd.
(415) 561-4323
offthegrid.com

TIP
Off the Grid and Presidio Trust also host Presidio Twilight on Thursdays between mid-May and mid-September, from 5-9 p.m., with food trucks, live music, free outdoor games, and 30 lantern-lit cabanas and fire pits for a "picnic at dusk" feel.

ROLL UP YOUR SLEEVES
WITH CELEBRITY CHEF JOANNE WEIR

Whether you're a seasoned cook who wants to beef up your recipe repertoire or you're a beginner who's intimidated by the word "kitchen," Chef Joanne Weir is your resident guru. She comes from a family of cooks but honed her skills under the tutelage of Alice Waters at the famed Chez Panisse in Berkeley. She's also a James Beard Award-winning cookbook author and the star of several public television shows, including *Joanne Weir's Cooking Class* and *Joanne Weir's Cooking Confidence*. Her newest show, *Joanne Weir's Plates & Places*, began airing in 2018. When she's not dropping by her restaurant, Copita, in Sausalito, she's welcoming students into her San Francisco kitchen for hands-on classes that blend her love of Mediterranean cuisine with California ingredients plucked from local farmers markets.

joanneweir.com

TIP
Feed your wanderlust by taking one of Joanne's classes in Spain, Morocco, Italy, or Mexico.

BELLY UP
TO A HOTEL BAR

In San Francisco, hotel bars are having a moment, one we hope isn't fleeting, serving innovative and fresh cocktails in some of the city's hippest settings.

TIP
Don't skip the bar food at these places. It's really good.

OUR FAVORITE HOTEL BAR HAUNTS

The Douglas Room
Tilden Hotel
A laid-back spot for
creative cocktails.
345 Taylor St.
(415) 673-2322
thedouglasroom.com

The JCB Tasting Lounge
Ritz Carlton
A luxe lounge in the lobby
for small-batch wines from
Jean-Charles Boisset.
600 Stockton St.
(415) 872-7983
jcbcollection.com

Benjamin Cooper
Hotel G
Contemporary cocktails served
in a vintage atmosphere.
398 Geary St.
(415) 654-5061
benjamincoopersf.com

Redwood Room
Clift Hotel
Glamour spot opened in 1934,
featuring Venetian glass and
original redwood paneling.
495 Geary St.
(415) 775-4700
sonesta.com

The Big 4
The Scarlet Huntington
A classic for a reason atop
Nob Hill.
1075 California St.
(415) 474-5400
big4restaurant.com

Dirty Habit
Hotel Zelos
Robust libations, rare
whiskeys, and a heated
outdoor patio.
12 4th St.
(415) 348-1555
dirtyhabitsf.com

Gibson
Bijou Hotel
The hotel's art deco
restaurant hides this
inviting bar.
111 Mason St.
(415) 771-7709
gibsonsf.com

NOURISH YOUR NIGHT OWL
AT THE GRUBSTAKE DINER

San Francisco is many things, but the city that never sleeps? Not so much. For those looking for post-barhopping sustenance, finding an open restaurant in the city used to be as challenging as landing a parking spot. Things have come around (for late-night dining anyway), and nocturnal nourishment is easier than ever. For this 1927 diner, however, the wee hours are nothing new, and they've been a favorite of the drunk and disorderly for decades, thanks to a generous 4 a.m. closing time. Set inside an old lunch wagon with hand-painted murals of San Francisco, the Grubstake serves staples such as omelets, pancakes, burgers, and French fries, as well as a handful of Portuguese dishes that pay homage to former owner Fernando Santos's heritage.

1525 Pine St.
(415) 673-8268
sfgrubstake.com

FUN FACT
The Grubstake appeared in season two of Food Network's *Diners, Drive-Ins and Dives.*

MORE LATE-NIGHT DINING DENS

Nopa
Midnight weeknights, 1 a.m. Friday and Saturday
560 Divisadero St.
(415) 864-8643
nopasf.com

The Brazen Head
Daily until 2 a.m.
3166 Buchanan St.
(415) 921-7600
brazenheadsf.com

Orphan Andy's
Open 24/7
3991 17th St.
(415) 864-9795

TIKI TRIP
TO THE TONGA ROOM

You can hardly call yourself a San Franciscan until you have fulfilled at least one luau-theme-party fantasy at Tonga Room & Hurricane Bar, opened in 1945 inside the Fairmont Hotel on Nob Hill. It's as famous for its colorful and boozy concoctions served at the side of a blue "lagoon" (the Fairmont's former indoor pool) as it is for the rain showers, complete with thunder and lightning. Enjoy tiki hall-of-famers such as the 1944 Mai Tai, Fog Cutter, Jet Pilot, and Jungle Bird while listening to the Island Groove Band, which plays on a floating stage.

950 Mason St.
(415) 772-5278
tongaroom.com

FUN FACT
Despite its clout at tiki bars everywhere, the Mai Tai cocktail was allegedly invented by a man named Victor Bergeron, who founded the original Trader Vic's in Emeryville, just across the bay.

USE BRUNCH AS A NOUN AND A VERB

If you spend even a short amount of time in San Francisco, you'll find out that brunch is both what you do and what you eat on weekend mornings. Locals take it seriously, and so do the many restaurants that cater to this San Francisco sport.

FUN FACT
Brunch originated in England in the late nineteenth century and became popular in the United States during the 1930s.

BRUNCH BEAT

Boogaloos
Back after a two-year closure,
with its beloved spud menu,
hash and eggs, and big
ol' biscuits served in a
former pharmacy.
3296 22nd St. (at Valencia)
(415) 824-4088
boogaloossf.com

The Ramp
A nothing-fancy outdoor
hangout in a former bait shop
on the waterfront.
855 Terry Francois St.
(415) 621-2378
rampsf.com

Outerlands
Near the beach, with a menu
of worth-the-wait-food,
including a Dutch pancake
baked in a cast iron pan.
4001 Judah St.
(415) 661-6140
outerlandssf.com

Old Devil Moon
Do the Black Magic Brunch
for great food and cocktails
that cast a spell.
3472 Mission St.
olddevilmoonsf.com

Zazie
Brunch daily on a menu with
seven kinds of eggs benny.
941 Cole St.
(415) 564-5332
zaziesf.com

EAT ROAST CHICKEN
AT ZUNI CAFÉ

This pie-shaped restaurant at Market and Rose Streets became an icon in 1987 when Chef Judy Rodgers came aboard and took Zuni from neighborhood hangout to San Francisco institution with a kitchen mantra of simple, local, and seasonal ingredients. Zuni Café would go on to win the James Beard Foundation Award for Outstanding Restaurant in the country in 2003, and in 2004, Judy won the James Beard Foundation Award for Outstanding Chef. When she took over Zuni, she requested that a brick oven and mesquite grill be put in the restaurant. The two-story behemoth is where Zuni's now-famous roast chicken for two is cooked. Simply seasoned with salt and pepper and served with a warm bread salad with scallions and mustard greens, the chicken is, more than three decades later, still the most popular item on the menu—proof positive that the simplest things are often the best. Judy passed away in 2013, but her spirit and recipes live on.

1658 Market St.
(415) 552-2522
zunicafe.com

TIP
The chicken takes an hour to prepare. Order a bottle of wine, relax, and enjoy the Zuni experience.

● ●

GET THAT OLD-SCHOOL STEAK HOUSE FEEL
AT THE HOUSE OF PRIME RIB

The restaurant is as jam-packed today as it was when it first opened in 1949, and the reason is simple: meat. The corn-fed beef is aged for twenty-one days, then roasted in coarse rock salt. The marbled prime rib is transferred to stainless steel carts and wheeled table to table, where a man in a tall white toque carves your perfect slice. Add to the picture white linen tablecloths and comforting side dishes such as the baked potato with all the fixings, sautéed spinach, homemade horseradish, and a salad, tossed tableside, and you'll swear you've time-machined back to your grandparents' favorite steak joint. Not to miss is their good, strong martini, which is almost as famous as the prime rib.

1906 Van Ness Ave.
(415) 885-4605
houseofprimerib.net

TIP
For non-carnivores, there is a hearty roasted vegetable plate and creamed corn.

QUEUE UP FOR SEAFOOD
AT SWAN OYSTER DEPOT

We know waiting in line is not fun, but it's what happens at restaurants around the city, and anyone who's any kind of seafood lover has done it at least once at Swan Oyster Depot. The one-hundred-plus-year-old fish market and restaurant is tiny, only eighteen stools along a Formica counter, but it manages to pack in locals, tourists, and even celebrities such as Bing Crosby, who once dined here, and Anthony Bourdain, who cracked crabs and jokes at Swan Oyster Depot in 2015. The massive menu board offers oysters, fresh fish, and seafood, among other choices, but their best seller is the combo salad with bay shrimp, prawns, and a dollop of Dungeness crab meat on a bed of lettuce, drizzled in creamy Louie dressing. Though people line up for some of the best seafood in the city, they return for the warm welcome served up by the Sancimino family, who've been behind the counter since 1946.

1517 Polk St.
(415) 673-1101

FUN FACT
Many websites masquerading as Swan Oyster Depot dot com have come and gone, but the restaurant, proudly, does not have one.

CHEER FOR CHOCOLATE
AT GHIRARDELLI SQUARE

It might surprise you to learn that San Francisco is the birthplace of two of the oldest chocolate makers in America: Ghirardelli and Guittard. Both companies have their roots in California's Gold Rush, and both still make chocolate in the Bay Area today. The Ghirardelli Chocolate Company's sweet history began in 1852, making it the oldest continuously operating chocolate maker in America. The company moved to what is now Ghirardelli Square in 1893, then eventually moved out of the city in need of more space. However, you can still taste the chocolate maker's history at shops tucked into the various landmark buildings.

900 North Point St.
(415) 775-5500
ghirardellisq.com

Chocolate check list

Dandelion Chocolate
Tour a bean-to-bar, small-batch factory in the heart of the Mission.
740 Valencia St.
(415) 349-0942
dandelionchocolate.com

Recchiuti Confections
Michael Recchiuti, with his wife, Jacky, create many of their artistic confections using Guittard chocolate.
1 Ferry Building Marketplace, #30
(415) 834-9494
recchiuti.com

BUST YOUR GUT ON A MISSION-STYLE BURRITO
AT TAQUERIA LA CUMBRE

San Franciscans are addicted to Mexican cuisine (we might actually have guacamole running through our veins), so it's a good thing the city is loaded with places to fill up on tacos, enchiladas, salsa, and our beloved Mission-style burrito, which first became popular during the 1960s in the city's Latin-centric Mission District. So, what is the big deal? BIG is the key word. Mission-style burritos are a hulky alter ego of your average Mexican roll-up, filled with rice, beans, salsa, meat, lettuce, cheese, and guacamole. Taqueria La Cumbre claims to have invented the first behemoth burrito, and their carne asada is a must. But rivals claim theirs are better. You decide. We're happy to get caught in the Mission burrito crossfire.

515 Valencia St.
(415) 863-8205
taquerialacumbre.com

FUN FACT
The burrito was made popular by Northern Mexican and American gold miners.

MORE MISSION BURRITO JOINTS

El Faro
Is this burrito nirvana? Only one way to find out.
2399 Folsom St.
(415) 647-3716

Taqueria Cancun
A formidable contender in your Mission burrito quest.
2288 Mission St.
(415) 252-9560
taqueria-cancun.cafes-world.com

Taqueria El Farolito
If the long line of burrito seekers doesn't
convince you, nothing will.
2779 Mission St.
(415) 824-7877

EAT YOUR WAY
AROUND JAPANTOWN

One of only three official Japantowns in the United States, San Francisco's once spanned thirty blocks and was called Nihonjin-Machi, or "Japanese People's Town." After WWII, the neighborhood changed and shrank, but it still satisfies cravings for authentic Japanese food and culture.

TIP
The Japan Center Mall (opened in 1968 as the Japanese Cultural and Trade Center) is a treasure trove of authentic restaurants and shops.

JAPANTOWN JAUNT

Benkyodo

For more than one hundred years, this bakery has made mochi and manju by hand, and it once supplied the Japanese Tea Garden with fortune cookies.

1747 Buchanan St.
(415) 922-1244
benkyodocompany.com

Waraku

A contemporary izakaya with various ramen styles and small plates for sharing.

1638 Post St.
(415) 292-3388
warakuus.com

Mum's

Shabu-shabu (cook-it-yourself in a hot pot) since 1995.

1800 Sutter St.
(415) 931-6986
mumssf.com

Yasukochi's Sweet Stop

Inside the Super Mira Market, the bakery makes coffee crunch cake, a San Francisco treat first made by Blum's.

1790 Sutter St.
(415) 931-8165

Kiss Seafood

A cozy space with twelve seats serving sushi, omakase, and other expertly prepared specialties.

1700 Laguna St.
(415) 474-2866
kissseafoodsf.com

CRACK SOME DUNGENESS CRAB

Come mid-November, markets, restaurant menus, and friends'
dinner tables overflow with San Francisco's beloved delicacy—
Dungeness crab. Though named for a small fishing village in
Washington, the six-legged crustacean is the undisputed king
of seafood around here, and practically the city's mascot. Some
say the holidays are the most wonderful time of the year, but for
seafood lovers, Dungeness crab season is tops.

TIP
Head to the stalls along Fisherman's Wharf for fresh crab
to eat on the spot or to go.

GET CRACKIN'

Anchor Oyster Bar

Steamed, chilled, or with garlic butter, the crab is always good
at this family-owned Castro gem.

579 Castro St.

(415) 431-3990

anchoroysterbar.com

Crustacean

An entire crab roasted with garlic and spices. Yes, please!

1475 Polk St.

(415) 776-2722

crustaceansf.com

PPQ Dungeness Island

Come November you have plenty of choices at
this unfussy crab crib.

2332 Clement St.

(415) 386-8266

ppqcrab.com

BLOW OFF SOME STEAM
AT ANCHOR BREWING

Like many San Francisco stories, Anchor Brewing's once-upon-a-time began during the California Gold Rush, and it is the only local brewery that has survived from that era. Though it was born under a different name near the turn of the century, the Anchor Brewing Company thrives today thanks to Frederick Louis "Fritz" Maytag III, who purchased a failing facility in 1965 and turned it into today's nationally recognized brand. Anchor is America's first and oldest craft brewery, with beers handmade from an all-malt mash in traditional copper kettles. Take a guided public tour, offered every day by reservation only. The tour starts in the taproom, with a beer in hand, where you'll get a brief history of the company from an Anchor employee before taking a stroll through three floors of the brewery. For more beers, go across the street to Anchor Public Taps, the company's new pilot brewery and taproom.

1705 Mariposa St.
(415) 863-8350
anchorbrewing.com

TIP
Children are welcome on the tour, but must be at least twenty-one years old to taste beer.

PICK UP THE PERFECT LOAF
AT TARTINE BAKERY

Drive by the corner of 18th and Guerrero Streets in the Mission District and there's always a line. No, they are not giving away free money inside. San Franciscans are instead waiting for one of Tartine's 240 perfect loaves of country sourdough bread, which are pulled from the oven from 5 p.m. until whenever they sell out, usually within the hour. Needless to say, Tartine is more than just a bakery in San Francisco—it's a bread blockbuster, created by baker Chad Robertson and his pastry chef wife, Elisabeth Prueitt, who've won James Beard awards for their craft. If sweets are more your style, you're in luck. Mornings at Tartine are infused with the aroma of irresistible and buttery baked goods such as perfect croissants, sugar-encrusted morning buns, and a delicate lemon cream tart that looks almost too beautiful to eat. Almost.

600 Guerrero St.
(415) 487-2600
tartinebakery.com

TIP
At the recently opened Tartine Manufactory restaurant, bar, and coffee shop, you can preorder your bread.
595 Alabama St., (415) 757-0007

SIP A CUPPA
AT THE JAPANESE TEA GARDEN

Tea is an ancient elixir enjoyed across continents, cultures, and centuries, and there are plenty of places in San Francisco to enjoy a good cuppa, including at the oldest public Japanese garden in the United States. Originally built as a "Japanese Village" for the California Midwinter International Exposition of 1894, the oasis in Golden Gate Park has paths, pruned plants, a pagoda, and a cozy teahouse overlooking a pond. It's the perfect place to zen out in the middle of the city. Choose from several Japanese snacks and varieties of tea including sencha, hojicha, and matcha. The Japanese Tea Garden was the first place in the U.S.A. to serve sweet fortune cookies as we know them, first made by Japantown's Benkyodo.

75 Hagiwara Tea Garden Dr.
(415) 752-1171
japaneseteagardensf.com

TIP
The teahouse now gets its fortune cookie supplies from Mee Mee Bakery (1328 Stockton St.) in Chinatown, where you can also visit Golden Gate Fortune Cookie Factory (56 Ross Alley) and watch the sweet treats get filled and folded before your eyes.

EARN TEQUILA BRAGGING RIGHTS
AT TOMMY'S MEXICAN RESTAURANT

Tommy's Mexican Restaurant has been around since 1965, when Elmy and Tomas Bermejo began serving food to hungry San Franciscans eager to taste Yucatán recipes. But what's tucked away behind the dining room is the real story here. The restaurant's bar, aka the best tequila spot in town, is where you'll find Julio, Elmy and Tomas's son, extolling the virtues of 100 percent-agave tequila. When he's not traveling to distilleries in Mexico or earning his spot on The World's 50 Best Bars list, he's furthering his tequila smarts and ours. His Blue Agave Club, now more than eight thousand members strong, invites the tequila curious to work their way through various levels including Tequila Master, PhD, Ninja Master, and Demigod/Demigoddess, while tasting some top-notch tequila. The best part of this "school" might just be the homework.

5929 Geary Blvd.
(415) 387-4747
tommysmexican.com

TIP
This is also the birthplace of the Tommy's Margarita. Don't miss it.

GOBBLE UP
A TASTE OF HISTORY
AT RED'S JAVA HOUSE

In a city where healthy food and cleanses are de rigueur, Red's Java House is proudly not the place to find them. You won't find vegetables on your sourdough-swaddled burger—just look closely at the menu that says "No lettuce, no tomato." What you do get, however, is a bite of San Francisco history inside a plucked-from-yesteryear shack on the waterfront. Back in the 1930s, the place was called Franco's Lunch and was a midday eatery for longshoremen. It was along these docks that Tom "Red" McGarvey sold copies of the local paper. In 1955, along with his brother Mike, Red bought Franco's and christened it with its new crimson name. With only a few exceptions, not much has changed over the decades, and that's just the way loyal Red's customers prefer to keep it.

Embarcadero, Pier 30
(415) 777-5626
redsjavahouse.com

TIP
There's a bar and patio out back that are not visible from the street.

SAY CHEESE
AT THE CHEESE SCHOOL
OF SAN FRANCISCO

America's only independent cheese school has been minding its curds and whey for more than a decade in San Francisco and recently relocated to a light and airy space at Ghirardelli Square—a delight for cheese and chocolate lovers alike. Check out their year-round schedule of classes that teach you everything you didn't know you needed to know about cheese, such as how to sniff Brie, what cheese to pair with wine and beer, mozzarella making, and much more. The school's snazzy new digs also have a retail store and café with cheese-focused dishes.

2124 Folsom St.
(415) 346-7530
thecheeseschool.com

MUSIC AND ENTERTAINMENT

ENJOY THE KITSCHY FUN
AT *BEACH BLANKET BABYLON*

The quirk, the color, the kitsch, the fun—it's what's made this San Francisco original the longest-running musical revue in the world. The whimsical, over-the-top show has been a mainstay in the city since 1974 and is a must for first-timers and locals who haven't seen it in a while, thanks to the script's perpetually updated narrative and a revolving door of super-sized hats and political and pop culture characters. *Beach Blanket Babylo*n was the brainchild of the late Steve Silver, whose vision of folding national headlines into a wacky stage performance that plays out as Snow White trying to find her Prince Charming was a clear formula for success. Audiences don't disagree and never seem to tire of the sidesplitting, laugh-out-loud fun that unfurls five nights a week at the legendary Club Fugazi in North Beach, on a part of Green Street renamed Beach Blanket Babylon Boulevard in 1996 in honor of the blockbuster.

678 Green St.
(415) 421-4222
beachblanketbabylon.com

TIP
While you must be over twenty-one to attend most shows, younger guests can enjoy BBB on Sundays.

ADMIRE AMERICA'S MUSIC
AT SFJAZZ

For longtime lovers of jazz or those curious to learn about the history of America's music, the thirty-five-thousand-square-foot SFJAZZ in Hayes Valley is a do-not-miss. Opened in January 2013, the cultural center has been called one of the greatest jazz concert halls in the world and is the first freestanding theater for jazz performance and education in America. Tune in for concerts, learn about jazz history from its African American roots to its modern expressions and interpretations, and attend events such as the annual SFJAZZ Festival. Drop into B-Side, a full-service restaurant and bar with a lounge-like vibe and of course, great music.

201 Franklin St.
(866) 920-5299
sfjazz.org

TIP
Check out the lobby's second floor murals called
Jazz and the Nation and *Jazz and the City*.

LISTEN TO GREAT BANDS
AT A MUSIC FESTIVAL

San Francisco cools down during the summer months, but the music is hot year-round, especially at the myriad of music festivals that invite you to swing, sing, and sway to some amazing tunes.

TIP
Consider public transport. Parking is near impossible on festival days.

MUSIC FESTIVAL LINE-UP

Noise Pop Festival

Twelve days of indie music and entertainment at stages around the Bay Area during February and March.
noisepopfest.com

SFJAZZ Festival

Top musicians from around the world come to San Francisco for two weeks each June.
sfjazz.org

Fillmore Jazz Festival

The Fillmore Jazz Festival is the largest free jazz event on the West Coast and takes place the first weekend in July on Fillmore Street.
sresproductions.com

Outside Lands

Each August, San Francisco's largest music festival brings sixty-five to seventy famous and local bands to Golden Gate Park for three days.
sfoutsidelands.com

Hardly Strictly Bluegrass

The popular Hardly Strictly Bluegrass is totally free, with large acts on stage each day during the first weekend of October in Golden Gate Park.
hardlystrictlybluegrass.com

Stern Grove Festival

Free concerts featuring world-class artists in a stunning outdoor amphitheater every Sunday from mid-June to mid-August.
sterngrove.org

PLAY A GAME
AT MUSÉE MÉCANIQUE

Appealing to the inner child in all of us, Musée Mécanique is one of the world's largest privately owned collections of mechanical and antique arcade machines, and nowhere else in the city can a pocket full of quarters provide hours of retro fun. Try your hand at more than three hundred coin-operated games including fortune tellers, love testers, skee ball, player pianos, a photo booth, pinball machines, air hockey tables, arm wrestling, and even an interlude with good old Laffing Sal, a six-foot-tall laughing automaton. Many of the games inside were once a part of the now defunct Playland at the Beach, a ten-acre amusement park next to San Francisco's Ocean Beach.

Pier 45, Fisherman's Wharf
(415) 346-2000
museemecaniquesf.com

TIP
Admission is free, but most machines cost twenty-five to
seventy-five cents to operate.

GET INTO THE ACT
AT A.C.T.

Movies are fine and fun, but watching live actors perform their hearts out is exhilarating, and in San Francisco, the American Conservatory Theater is where to witness the craft in top form. The nonprofit company is the city's premier live theater outfit, performing a run of classical and contemporary productions each year at historic Geary Theater, built in 1910 and originally called the Columbia Theater. In 2015, A.C.T. expanded by opening the 283-seat Strand Theater with basement cabaret, acting workshops, and productions connected to their highly competitive MFA program that admits only eight students per year. A.C.T. was the first theater to win a Tony Award for the quality of its training program as well as its performances. A.C.T. was also the first independent theater in the nation to win academic accreditation and the authority to grant a master of fine arts in acting.

405 Geary St.
(415) 749-2228
act-sf.org

FUN FACT
Actress Annette Bening was a member of the acting company at A.C.T. while studying at San Francisco State University.

GET UP CLOSE TO AQUATIC LIFE
AT THE AQUARIUM OF THE BAY

On the water's edge at Pier 39, twenty thousand sea creatures from the San Francisco Bay and the surrounding water await. You'll come eye to eye with a sevengill shark, watch the hypnotic motion of the moon jellies, and even touch a bat ray's wing. You'll have the illusion of being under the sea as you walk through transparent tunnels that bring the diverse aquatic life up close. There are also daily naturalist-led animal feedings; talks about jellyfish, tide pools, and octopi; and interactive science experiments. Though not found under the sea, otters are considered a watershed ambassador, as they are indicators of healthy waterways, and the Aquarium of the Bay is home to four of these adorable residents.

Embarcadero at Beach St.
(415) 623-5300
bayecotarium.org

TIP
Add a Behind-the-Scenes Tour or Feed-the-Sharks Tour to your general admission ticket. Book online.

SING ALONG
AT THE CASTRO THEATRE

This single-screen movie house on Castro Street and in the neighborhood of the same name is not just one of San Francisco's most beloved landmarks—it's also one of the country's oldest operating movie theaters. Built in 1922, the Castro Theatre was commissioned by the Nasser brothers, who came from a large movie-business family in San Francisco. The Spanish Colonial exterior was designed to evoke a Mexican cathedral, while inside it's all fantasy and magic, with tassels, swags, and a ceiling that looks like leather. The Nassers leased the theater to a large corporation during the 1970s but took back ownership in 2001, making substantial improvements to the theater's 1,400 seats as well as to the sound and screen technologies. While it's a fantastic place to take in mainstream movies, indie and foreign films, and double features, the sing-alongs to classics such as *Grease* and *The Sound of Music* are the theater's most popular attraction.

429 Castro St.
(415) 621-6120
castrotheatre.com

TIP
Costumes are not just welcome but encouraged at sing-alongs.

ROCK OUT
ON ROCK HISTORY
AT THE FILLMORE

There are concert venues across the country, but few are as legendary as The Fillmore Auditorium. Known simply as The Fillmore, the one-thousand-person hall, first opened in 1912, has had several lives, including as a dance hall, a roller skating rink, and a private club. But it was a successful African American businessman named Charles Sullivan who started booking bands here in the 1950s. He renamed the venue for the neighborhood, but little did he know that the name would be forever linked to rock promoter Bill Graham, who began hosting rock bands during the mid-1960s. Among the epic San Francisco-based musicians who cut their teeth at The Fillmore were the Grateful Dead, Santana, Jefferson Airplane, Big Brother and the Holding Company featuring Janis Joplin. Other marquee names, including The Doors, The Who, Pink Floyd, Fleetwood Mac, and Led Zeppelin, to name only a few, have also walked these hallowed halls.

1805 Geary Blvd.
(415) 346-6000
thefillmore.com

FOLLOW THE LOVE
WITH SAN FRANCISCO LOVE TOURS

Hitch a ride on a peace, love, and hippy-vibe tour of the city in vintage VW buses that bring the color of the 1960s and '70s along for the ride. Founded by two brothers in 2015 who love San Francisco, this tour is as informative as it is fun. Enjoy the buses' throwback decor of orange shag carpet and beaded curtains as well as hand-painted murals on the exterior that draw cheers and waves. Each bus holds only six people, who are regaled with fun facts and stories by a knowledgeable driver and guide. Book a two-hour tour for a trip to well-known San Francisco sites and neighborhoods, or charter a bus for yourself and five friends, and customize a memorable day around the city by the bay.

2899 Hyde St.
(415) 366-6156
sanfranciscolovetours.com

TIP
You can reserve tickets online, but cancellations must be made forty-eight hours in advance for a full refund.

BECOME A BALLET, OPERA, AND SYMPHONY FAN
AT THE WAR MEMORIAL OPERA & PERFORMING ARTS CENTER

The San Francisco Ballet, America's oldest classical ballet company, began as the San Francisco Operatic and Ballet School, founded by San Francisco Opera general director Gaetano Merola in 1933. Eventually the ballet and opera split into two companies. On Christmas Eve 1944, Tchaikovsky's *The Nutcracker* was performed by the San Francisco Ballet, marking the first time a complete version had ever been staged in the United States. Clara and the Sugar Plum Fairy still return to San Francisco each year to dazzle audiences young and old. If ballet and opera performances aren't your thing, don't miss a chance to hear the award-winning, world-class San Francisco Symphony that performs at the gorgeous Louise M. Davies Symphony Hall, just across the street.

301 Van Ness Ave.
(415) 621-6600
sfwmpac.org

FUN FACT
The original United Nations Charter was signed here on June 26, 1945.

EDUCATE YOUR NIGHTLIFE
AT THE CALIFORNIA ACADEMY
OF SCIENCES

The city's premier science museum, located in Golden Gate Park, invites cocktail lovers and science geeks to join forces at its weekly Thursday night cocktail party event. A different theme is planned for each night and can be anything from the secrets of animal migration to robots, and special programs somehow manage to educate the masses while keeping things fun. Guests can also check out the planetarium and aquarium, chat with scientists, and get up close to some of the museum's resident creatures, all under one living roof. There are multiple bars as well as music.

55 Music Concourse Dr.
(415) 379-8000
calacademy.org

TIP
This is a twenty-one-plus event, and a valid ID is required for entry.

SEE THE LIGHTS OF BROADWAY
AT THE ORPHEUM

Built in 1926 as a showcase for theater magnate Alexander Pantages, the SHN Orpheum Theatre (once called the Pantages) has welcomed vaudeville acts, silent films, motion pictures, and musical and theatrical entertainment troupes. These days, it's the place in San Francisco to see a Broadway hit, with six to seven of the biggest shows on the schedule every season. Acclaimed productions such as *The Lion King*, *The Book of Mormon*, and *Hamilton* earned standing ovations at the Orpheum. In addition to enjoying what's on stage, you can revel in the fact that you are doing so in a San Francisco Historical Landmark. The Orpheum Theatre, along with the historic Curran and Golden Gate Theatres, is owned and operated by SHN, a company dedicated to bringing Broadway road shows and pre-Broadway productions to all three stages. Before opening on Broadway, *Wicked* had its world premiere at the Curran in May 2003.

1192 Market St.
(888) 746-1799
shnsf.com

TIP
SHN Orpheum Theatre has partnered with Parking Panda to allow visitors to pre-purchase guaranteed parking near the theater.

GET YOUR MIND BLOWN
AT THE MARRAKECH MAGIC THEATER

Sleight-of-hand virtuoso, mind-reading wizard, master of astonishing tricks, amazing mentalist, and really hilarious comic Jay Alexander will blow your mind four nights a week at this intimate theater near Union Square. He's one of the top corporate and society entertainers in the country, and some of his notable appearances include the *TODAY* show and *Good Morning America*. Jay has also given special performances for U2 front man Bono, as well as the late Robin Williams. As a child, Jay found a trunk in his grandparents' attic full of magical apparatus and escape illusions, a discovery that launched his magical curiosity. At the age of fourteen, Jay was the youngest recipient of the Society of American Magicians' Gold Medal of Honor. Since then, audiences around the world have been wondering the same thing: "How did he do that?!" Come see if you can figure it out.

419 O'Farrell St.
(415) 794-6893
sanfranciscomagictheater.com

TIP
The show is family friendly for children ages eight and up.

RISE UP FOR THE CLASSICAL REVOLUTION
AT THE REVOLUTION CAFE

Classical Revolution was founded in the fall of 2006 by local musician Charith Premawardhana, who envisioned moving classical music performances from stuffy concert halls to a more fun, laid-back, and accessible environment by way of neighborhood cafés and galleries. Since its successful first year of weekly shows at Revolution Cafe in San Francisco's Mission District, the organization has grown exponentially and registered as a nonprofit, and it still brings classical music to the neighborhood where it all began. Stop by the Revolution Cafe for different featured musicians every first and third Monday.

3248 22nd St.
(415) 642-0474
classicalrevolution.com

TIP
Music is presented free of charge, but a five- to twenty-dollar donation is appreciated.

BECOME A FILM BUFF
AT THE SAN FRANCISCO
INTERNATIONAL FILM FESTIVAL

Hollywood might be a few hundred miles south, but San Francisco is no stranger to great film. Founded in 1957 and rolling out for two weeks each spring, the San Francisco International Film Festival is the longest-running film festival in the Americas. More than 180 films are shown on screens around the Bay Area, including at San Francisco's beloved Castro Theatre. There are also live events, and as many as one hundred filmmakers attend in hopes of capturing one of the nearly two dozen awards presented for excellence in craft. The festival is put on by SFFILM, a nonprofit organization delivering screenings and events as well as media education programs to more than ten thousand students and teachers each year. Join and get best access to the SFFILM Festival, as well as invitations to free screenings throughout the year.

(414) 561-5000
sffilm.org

TIP
Download the SFFILM app on your smartphone
for lineups and show times at your fingertips.

TAKE A WHIRL
ON THE GOLDEN GATE PARK CAROUSEL

Carousels are part of a magical childhood memory that many of us can recall—a timeless, nostalgic, and old-fashioned type of fun that's becoming lost on today's technology-addicted kids. Luckily, the Koret Children's Quarter in Golden Gate Park has a 1914 Herschell–Spillman gem that will spark young imaginations anew thanks to a menagerie of colorful creatures, music, and lights.

320 Bowling Green Dr.
(415) 831-2700
goldengatepark.com

More fun twirls

Dentzel Carousel
San Francisco Zoo has one of the world's last existing machines handcrafted by William H. Dentzel.
Sloat Blvd. at the Great Hwy.
(415) 753-7080
sfzoo.org

LeRoy King Carousel
Children's Creativity Museum, constructed in 1906 by famed designer Charles I. D. Looff.
221 4th St.
(415) 820-3320
creativity.org

San Francisco Carousel
Pier 39 has a sea creature theme and is painted with famous San Francisco landmarks.
Pier 39, Fisherman's Wharf

TIP

Make a special occasion out of it by calling to reserve the picnic area adjacent to the Golden Gate Park carousel.

SHOW YOUR LOVE FOR THE WRITTEN WORD
AT LITQUAKE

San Francisco's vibrant literary scene is celebrated every day, but the bookish heat boils in October when this popular nine-day-and-night festival invites writers to share their work all around the city. For attendees, this means mostly free events at bars, bookstores, boutiques, and galleries where authors, poets, storytellers, teachers, editors, and other literati share their words and craft. Originally hatched in 1999 as an afternoon of free readings in Golden Gate Park, Litquake quickly morphed and grew to become a San Francisco literary juggernaut that lures local, national, and international wordsmiths. Best of all, Litquake is a nonprofit organization actively supporting the love of reading, writing, and books across San Francisco's diverse communities.

(415) 440-4177
litquake.org

TIP
If you can only make one night, go for Lit Crawl, the final evening of the festival, which counts more than one hundred literary events around the Mission District.

TO BE OR NOT TO BE
AT SHAKESPEARE IN THE PARK

The San Francisco Shakespeare Festival is best known for its annual Shakespeare in the Park production, which travels to five different Bay Area venues between July and October, including to the city, at the Presidio and in John McLaren Park's Jerry Garcia Amphitheatre during the month of September. The festival began in 1983 with its debut production of *The Tempest* in Golden Gate Park. Shakespeare in the Park is free of charge, which means you can bring your entire family plus friends, pack a picnic, and enjoy the theater. We think the Bard of Avon would love it.

Presidio Main Post Lawn
210 Lincoln Blvd.
(415) 558-0888
sfshakes.org

TIP
No seating is provided at the Presidio, but blankets and low chairs (no more than six inches off the ground) are welcome.

GO OLD SCHOOL GLAM
AT THE STARLIGHT ROOM

You haven't really experienced San Francisco until you've taken the elevator twenty-one floors up to the top of the Sir Francis Drake Hotel and watched the city twinkle beneath your toes. It sets the mood for a night to remember, as do the plush red interior and cozy booths that recall a bygone era. The music has changed since the Starlight Room first opened in 1928, but resident DJs keep you hopping six nights a week. On Tuesdays, count on live jazz from 7 to 10 p.m. Sign up for the popular "Sunday's A Drag" brunch for a diva-licious San Francisco original. The nightclub and cocktail lounge received a facelift in 2011, but she remains as glamorous as ever.

450 Powell St.
(415) 395-8595
starlightroomsf.com

TIP
There is a dress code for ladies and gents, which means you should dress to impress and not for the beach.

GET A MENTAL TUNE-UP
AT THE WAVE ORGAN

Out on a jetty in the Marina district of San Francisco, the Wave Organ was built in 1986 in collaboration with the Exploratorium, which was formerly housed nearby in the Palace of Fine Arts. The hands-on science museum has since moved to Pier 15, but the wave-activated sculpture of granite and marble (rumor has it that it was sourced from a demolished cemetery) remains to enchant visitors. Artist Peter Richards created the masterpiece that amplifies sound as waves roll in and crash against the twenty pipes that extend into the water. The cacophony is what you'd expect of a liquid symphony—sometimes gurgling and rumbling, often whooshing and swishing, and a balance of high- and low-pitched sounds that are as entertaining as they are contemplative. One thing is guaranteed—no tune will ever be the same and the views of Alcatraz and the Golden Gate Bridge never get old.

Pier 15, Embarcadero at Green St.
(415) 528-4444
exploratorium.edu

TIP
The musical marvels of the wave organ are best experienced at high tide.

SPORTS AND RECREATION

WALK THROUGH TIME
ON ANGEL ISLAND

Comprising the entirety of the largest island in San Francisco Bay, Angel Island State Park has hiking and bicycling trails, picnic and camping spots, and some of the most breathtaking views of San Francisco, Marin County, and the Golden Gate Bridge. It also has a rich cultural history. For the Coast Miwok, the island was a seasonal hunting and gathering location. Spanish explorer Juan Manuel de Ayala used Angel Island as a safe refuge and supply stop when he mapped the San Francisco Bay. For nearly one hundred years—from the Civil War to the Cold War—the federal government used its strategic location for military bases, a quarantine station, and an immigration station. You can reach Angel Island year-round by public ferries: Blue & Gold Ferry Service when coming from San Francisco, Oakland, and Alameda; Angel Island Ferry Service when coming from Tiburon. A number of agencies offer organized Segway tours, hiking tours, and other ways to discover the island, but you're free to explore on your own, too. The perimeter trail, a 5.5-mile loop around the island, is a top choice.

(415) 435-3392
angelisland.com

TIP

To snag one of the island's eleven coveted campsites on a weekend, book at least six months in advance. Campsite 4 has beautiful views, but direct exposure to wind and sun. Campsite 5 has a good vista and is a little more protected.

RUN THE BAY
TO BREAKERS
(WITH OR WITHOUT A COSTUME)

If there's one event in San Francisco that shows the most concrete evidence of the city's free spirit, it's the annual Bay to Breakers footrace. Established in 1912 as the Cross City Race, it was a way to lift civic morale after the 1906 San Francisco earthquake and fire. The twelve-kilometer (7.46-mile) race from the San Francisco Bay to the breakers of the Pacific Ocean isn't only for serious runners. It's especially known for some participants' extravagant and eclectic costumes and other participants' lack of any costume whatsoever (cover your eyes, kids!). As runners and walkers make their way up Hayes Street Hill, along the Panhandle, and through Golden Gate Park, live music, the cheers of spectators, and the irrepressible audacity of fellow San Franciscans energize them. The race is typically held the third Sunday in May.

Main St. at Howard St.
(415) 231-3130
baytobreakers.com

TIP

While the Bay to Breakers has a history of luring naked runners as well as those who sport elaborate costumes, be aware that San Francisco does have a law banning public nudity, and it's up to the police department whether it is enforced on Bay to Breakers days.

TAKE YOURSELF OUT TO THE BALL GAME
AT AT&T PARK

The smell of freshly cut grass, the crack of the bat—it must be baseball season, and there's no better place to be than at San Francisco's AT&T Park, home to the San Francisco Giants. Opened on April 11, 2000, AT&T Park replaced the Giants' former home, Candlestick Park—a windy, multiuse sports park that the Giants shared with the San Francisco 49ers. The new park was engineered to have less than half the wind interference. Meet your friends at the Willie Mays statue and grab a pregame drink at Public House. Inside the park, the dining choices are what you'd expect from a food-crazed city. Grab anything from pizza to hot dogs, pulled-pork sandwiches to Mission-style burritos, clam chowder to crab sandwiches, fresh salads, and more. Find your seat, settle in, and root, root, root for the home team!

24 Willie Mays Plaza
(415) 972-2000
sanfrancisco.giants.mlb.com

TIP
At the end of the game, don't rush to leave. If the Giants win, you can soak in the happy mood while listening to Tony Bennett serenade the crowd with "I Left My Heart in San Francisco."

CATCH SOME AIR
AT HOUSE OF AIR

If you've long envied birds and other flying creatures, take a terrestrial trip to the historic airplane hangar at Crissy Field to find a temporary fix. The indoor trampoline park has three high-performance trampolines and two recreational areas enclosed within padded walls and patched with more than sixty conjoined trampolines, as well as a bounce house for small children. Inside the two trampoline arenas, adults and kids aged seven and older can aimlessly catapult into the air to their heart's content. Regular "air conditioning classes" are available for those who want to spend some dedicated time in the air. Whether your airborne dream includes open trampoline jump time, aerial and physical training, trampoline dodgeball, trampoline basketball dunking, ninja obstacle courses, or regular air conditioning classes—all of them give you the temporary gift of flight.

926 Mason St.
(415) 345-9675
houseofair.com

FUN FACT
Trampolining made its first appearance as an Olympic sport at the 2000 Summer Games in Sydney, Australia.

PRACTICE YOGA
AT GRACE CATHEDRAL

Imagine doing your downward dog to live music on a labyrinth among hundreds of people in a darkened cathedral. That's exactly what yoga night (on Tuesday) at Grace Cathedral is about—meeting people where they are and recognizing that there are many ways to be spiritual. The cathedral is home to two labyrinths—one indoors (a replica of the medieval labyrinth of Chartres Cathedral in France) and one outdoors. Yoga class is held indoors from 6:15 to 7:30 p.m. and is so popular that yoga mats spread across the labyrinth, the aisles, and even the altar (it's a smart move to show up early). The class is free, but a ten- to twenty-dollar donation is suggested to support the teacher, musicians, and cathedral. Grace Cathedral, the third-largest Episcopal cathedral in the United States, is a renowned San Francisco landmark and a regional magnet where diverse people come to celebrate, find solace, and connect with others.

1100 California St.
(415) 749-6300
gracecathedral.org

TIP
Outdoor Yoga SF (outdooryogasf.com) also holds
yoga classes in iconic San Francisco locations.

BARK WITH THE SEA LIONS
AT K-DOCK

Pier 39's K-Dock hasn't always been home to boisterous, barking California sea lions. Shortly after the 1989 Loma Prieta earthquake, the playful pinnipeds began hauling out at K-Dock, and their numbers grew from an initial fifty to an all-time record of 1,701 in November 2009. The cozy spot became ideal for the sea lions, due to the protective environment and a plentiful herring supply. For the animals, hauling out in between foraging activities provides a time of rest, thermoregulation, and reproduction. The number of sea lions at K-Dock will vary with the seasons, available food supply, and migration patterns, but it's often likely that someone's home. Weather permitting, volunteers from the Marine Mammal Center are around on Saturdays and Sundays from 11 a.m. to 5 p.m. to answer questions about the California sea lions. They also monitor K-Dock's sea lion population, so you're bound to get an accurate count from those in the know.

Beach St. at the Embarcadero
(415) 705-5500
pier39.com

TIP
The Sea Lion Center, overlooking K-Dock, sheds light on the animals' role in the San Francisco Bay ecosystem and has interactive displays, real sea lion artifacts, and educational videos.

TAKE IN THE VIEW
FROM TWIN PEAKS

For a lay of the land, the stunning 360-degree view from atop Twin Peaks is one of the best places to perch. Originally called Los Pechos de la Choca ("Breasts of the Maiden") by Spanish settlers, these two adjacent peaks provide a vista spanning from Ocean Beach and the Golden Gate Bridge to the Mission District and Potrero Hill. At 922 feet in elevation, Twin Peaks is second to Mount Richardson in height and gives visitors a glimpse at what San Francisco's hills may have looked like before grazing and development changed them. Whether you hike or drive to the summit, expect strong winds at the top and dress accordingly. Look up before you head up, because the weather at sea level may be very different than what's waiting for you up above.

501 Twin Peaks Blvd.
(415) 831-2700
sfrecpark.org/destination/twin-peaks

TIP
The grassland and coastal scrub that stretches over the park's sixty-four acres is home to the endangered Mission Blue Butterfly, as well as coyotes, brush rabbits, and white-crowned sparrows.

HEAR THE CALL
OF THE WILD PARROTS
ON TELEGRAPH HILL

One of San Francisco's original "Seven Hills," Telegraph Hill is known primarily for Coit Tower. But if you hear parrot squawks during your visit, don't be surprised. Telegraph Hill is also known for its flock of wild parrots. The flock itself began when a pair of escaped red-masked parakeets (also known as cherry-headed conures in the pet trade) made Telegraph Hill their home. The pair was joined by other escapees, and after a few generations, there are now more than three hundred of their descendants flying around San Francisco, with smaller flocks hanging out all over the city. If you're in search of the Telegraph Hill parrots, be prepared to walk the Filbert Street stairs. But take time to pause along the way to admire the gardens among the urban jungle. Even if you're not lucky enough to spy parrots, you'll likely hear their chatter.

Filbert St. at Kearny St.

TIP

For a glimpse into the early days of the flock, check out Mark Bittner's book, *The Wild Parrots of Telegraph Hill*, or the documentary film of the same name.

SOAK THE STRESS AWAY
AT KABUKI SPRINGS & SPA

An urban retreat in the heart of San Francisco's Japantown, Kabuki Springs & Spa keeps the tradition of Japanese public baths. The communal, clothing-optional baths include a hot pool (104 degrees), cold plunge (55 degrees), dry sauna (140 degrees), and steam room (120 degrees)—and it's difficult to leave the facility not changed for the better. The bath schedule is inclusive to everyone and alternates days for women (and trans women) and men (and trans men). All genders, including non-binary, are welcome on all-gender day, and bathing suits are required. Spa treatments are also offered, from a variety of massages and facials to body treatments influenced by traditional Asian bodywork, rituals, and ceremonies. Packages are available, and the spa staff is always generous with advice on how best to focus on your desired Kabuki experience.

1750 Geary Blvd.
(415) 922-6000
kabukisprings.com

TIP
Communal bathing fees are discounted when you also book a treatment, so make it a spa day and revel in the relaxation.

RUN AWAY TO JOIN THE CIRCUS
AT CIRCUS CENTER

Fulfill childhood dreams of running away to the circus at the San Francisco Circus Center, one of the most advanced schools of the circus arts on the West Coast, where entry level to advanced classes is offered in flying trapeze, acrobatics, aerial arts, contortion, juggling, trampoline, and many other disciplines. Begun in 1984 as the San Francisco School for Circus Arts by founders of the Pickle Family Circus, the school was renamed Circus Center in 2001. It has become known for its quality training from a world-renowned team of instructors that have performed with the Nanjing Acrobatic Troupe, Moscow Circus, Cirque du Soleil, Pickle Family Circus, Circus Bella, Circus Smirkus, Teatro ZinZanni, Ringling Bros. and Barnum & Bailey, and the Big Apple Circus.

755 Frederick St.
(415) 759-8123
circuscenter.org

TIP
If you're more an aficionado than an acrobat, consider attending The Circus Center Cabaret, featuring the best of Bay Area circus talent.

PICNIC
AT INA COOLBRITH PARK

On the east side of Russian Hill, Vallejo Street becomes too steep for cars and ends abruptly at a compact green space with winding paths, benches, and breathtaking views. Named for Ina Coolbrith, a prominent figure in the early San Francisco literary scene and California's first poet laureate, the park, which was dedicated by Coolbrith supporters in 1911, feels like a hidden green space in the city. It also has some of the best views in San Francisco, but access is uphill, so be prepared to work for them. Your reward is a lookout over Chinatown and the Financial District, the Bay Bridge, Coit Tower, and the Transamerica Pyramid. From the "Poet's Corner," Alcatraz and Angel Island lie to the north.

Vallejo St. at Taylor St.
(415) 831-5500
sfrecpark.org/destination/ina-coolbrith-park

FUN FACT
Ina Coolbrith is buried in Mountain View Cemetery in Oakland, just across the bay.

ZIP DOWN
THE SEWARD STREET SLIDES

Most slides in playgrounds across San Francisco beckon children, while adults watch from the sidelines. But the slides at the Seward Mini Park sound a siren call to all children at heart, as long as they're wearing sturdy pants and carry a piece of cardboard. This park owes its existence to dedicated residents who sat in protest against the disappearance of open space and a developer's bulldozers. In the end, they triumphed, and the Seward Mini Park opened in 1973. Home to a community garden and a collection of native plants, it's especially known for the long, steep concrete slides designed by fourteen-year-old Kim Clark. Signs dictate that adults must be accompanied by a child in order to ride the two curvy, side-by-side slides. The park is open from sunrise to sunset. Sorry, no midnight rides.

30 Seward St.
sfrecpark.org/destination/seward-mini-park

TIP
The cardboard not only hastens the downward descent on the slides, but also keeps your clothing from tearing like wet paper.

CHOOSE YOUR ADVENTURE
AT A SAN FRANCISCO BEACH

Bordered by water on three sides, San Francisco has no shortage of beaches. While you're more likely to see people bundled up in hoodies than board shorts, these coastal spots bring out brave surfers and kite flyers, and anyone who enjoys a walk in the sand and spectacular views. Just west of the Golden Gate Bridge, mile-long **Baker Beach** is a big favorite of locals and visitors alike, thanks to views of the iconic bridge and the Marin Headlands. FYI: the northernmost part of the beach (often referred to as **Marshall's Beach**) is clothing optional. The small cove between Baker Beach and Lands End is home to **China Beach**, named after Chinese fishermen from the Gold Rush era who camped here on the sand. Fort Funston lies below the two-hundred-foot-high bluffs and is where romping pups, strolling couples, horseback riders, and hang gliders flock. San Francisco's largest and most popular beach, **Ocean Beach**, stretches for 3.5 miles on the far west of the city and is favored by bonfire fans and surfers braving the dangerous rip currents.

Baker Beach
1504 Pershing Dr.

China Beach
340 Sea Cliff Ave.

Fort Funston
Skyline Blvd. and John Muir Dr.

Lands End
680 Point Lobos Ave.

Ocean Beach
Great Hwy. between Geary Blvd. and Sloat Blvd.
nps.gov/goga

DO IT ALL
AT YERBA BUENA GARDENS

This urban respite lies in the heart of San Francisco's downtown cultural district and is packed with landscaped gardens, public art, a performing arts center, galleries, shops, theaters, museums, and restaurants; a historic carousel; ice skating and bowling centers; and award-winning architecture. Yerba Buena was the original name of the settlement that became San Francisco. Spanish for "good herb," yerba buena is a low-growing, perennial member of the mint family that is native to the area. A haven for families, Yerba Buena is considered one of the top thirty urban parks in the nation. Try your hand at interactive activities at the Children's Creativity Museum, play in the Children's Garden, whirl around on the LeRoy King Carousel, get some time on the ice at the Yerba Buena Ice Skating + Bowling Center, see the newest blockbuster film at Metreon, and attend a performance at Yerba Buena Center for the Arts.

750 Howard St.
(415) 820-3550
yerbabuenagardens.com

TIP
Between May and October, the Yerba Buena Gardens Festival presents more than seventy-five free performances, including music, dance, theater, cultural events, and educational and children's programs.

GET TWISTY
ON SAN FRANCISCO'S CROOKED STREETS

Surrounded by mansions and meticulously landscaped yards, the eight hairpin turns on Russian Hill's Lombard Street (between Jones and Hyde Streets) have made it one of San Francisco's most popular landmarks and given it the universally known title of the "crookedest street in the world." The naturally steep grade of the street posed a serious safety hazard, and the switchbacks were proposed by a property owner to reduce speed on Lombard, which was too steep for most vehicles. Despite its nickname, Lombard Street isn't even the crookedest street in San Francisco. That honor goes to the two-block portion of Vermont Street in Potrero Hill. Vermont Street has only seven switchbacks to Lombard Street's eight, but the steepness of the street adds to its sinuosity—which is higher.

Lombard St. (between Jones St. and Hyde St.)
Vermont St. (between Twentieth St. and Twenty-Second St.)

TIP
The Bring Your Own Big Wheel race is held on Vermont Street each Easter, and it's open to both kids and adult drivers of Big Wheels or trikes that are made of plastic with plastic wheels.

BASK IN THE GLOW
OF THE GOLDEN GATE BRIDGE

Spanning almost two miles across the Golden Gate, the narrow strait where San Francisco Bay opens to meet the Pacific Ocean, the Golden Gate Bridge connects the city of San Francisco and Marin County, California. It took four years to build, at a cost of $35 million, and opened in 1937. The single suspension span is anchored by twin towers that have a height of 746 feet (above water level) and the two main cables measure 7,650 feet each, but each main cable is composed of 27,572 wires. If the wires were one continuous length, they could wrap around the Earth more than three times. Visitors can walk or bike the entire length of the bridge, but dress warmly, because wind can whip through the Golden Gate. If you're not game to walk, visit the vista points located on the north and south sides of the bridge.

(415) 921-5858
goldengatebridge.org

FUN FACT
Painting the bridge is an ongoing task and a primary maintenance job. The paint, a color called International Orange, protects the bridge's steel from the high salt content in the air and helps prevent corrosion and rust.

PEEK INTO THE CITY'S PAST
AT PRESIDIO

This fifteen-thousand-acre park, an essential part of the Golden Gate National Recreation Area, is also an essential part of the history of San Francisco. After serving as home to native peoples for thousands of years, the Presidio became a Spanish military fort in 1776. Mexico controlled the post after its independence from Spain in 1821, and soldiers and settlers established a pueblo nearby, called Yerba Buena. That pueblo grew into today's San Francisco. But the Presidio still had two more incarnations to come. It was a working U.S. Army base from 1846, before California was a state, until 1994. Since then, the Presidio has been part of the Golden Gate National Recreation Area. There's so much to do here that it helps to get oriented at the Presidio Visitor Center. Drop in to the Presidio Officers' Club to learn about the park's rich history. Beaches and coastal space abound from Baker Beach to Crissy Field—the sandy stretch that lures families, kiteboarders, and windsurfers. Many of the buildings that once housed military personnel have been turned into destinations open to the public, such as the Walt Disney Family Museum, a handful of restaurants, and a bowling center.

210 Lincoln Blvd.
(415) 561-4323
nps.gov/prsf, presidio.gov

PEOPLE WATCH
LIKE A SAN FRANCISCAN
AT MISSION DOLORES PARK

Named for nearby Mission Dolores, this sixteen-acre park is one of the city's most popular destinations. People of all shapes, sizes, ages, ethnicities, genders, and sexualities lounge on the lawn enjoying views of the city. Ohlone peoples were the first to inhabit this land; they later shared it with Spanish ranchers and shopkeepers after missionaries established Misión San Francisco de Asís. Shortly after the city bought the property and established the park, it served as a refugee camp for residents made homeless by the 1906 earthquake and fire. This vibrant heart of the city has a wealth of lush lawns, a soccer field, a basketball court, a multiuse court, a playground, two off-leash dog play zones, and six tennis courts. One of the best ways to enjoy Dolores Park, however, is to sit back and watch the parade of people.

Dolores St. at 19th St.
sfrecpark.org/destination/mission-dolores-park

FUN FACT
The fire hydrant at the top of the park (at Church and 20th Streets) has an important role in the history of the Mission District. After the 1906 earthquake and fire, it was the only working fire hydrant left in the area and saved the neighborhood from total destruction.

CLIMB THE STAIRWAYS TO HEAVEN

San Francisco is a city of hills that give rise to other landmarks, such as Coit Tower and cable cars "that climb halfway to the stars." And with hills, come the stairs—lots of them. Whether your workout goals include glute burning or merely spectacular views and fresh air, there's a staircase in the city for you. The wide and well-maintained **Lyon Street** steps lure fitness fanatics. The **16th Avenue** tiled stairs are a work of art, as are the mosaic steps in **Sea Cliff**, at the end of California Street. Steep-stairway seekers prefer the long continuous rise of the **Baker Street** steps, and extremists seek out the **Bernal Heights** neighborhood, with the most stairways in the hilly city. The windy **Filbert Street** stairs pass lush gardens that are home to the wild parrots of Telegraph Hill, the **Vallejo Street** stairs cut through Ina Coolbrith Park and are among the few large cobblestone staircases left in the city, and nearly all the houses along the **Vulcan Steps** are accessible only by foot.

TIP
One of the best ways to find San Francisco's stairways is in the book *Stairway Walks in San Francisco* by Adah Bakalinsky and Mary Burk.

WALK OR RUN
FROM CRISSY FIELD TO FORT POINT

The round-trip from Crissy Field to Fort Point measures just under two miles and offers amazing views of the Golden Gate Bridge, the Marin Headlands, and Alcatraz. Crissy Field was once a U.S. Army airfield, but it was transformed into one of the most popular recreation areas in the city, opening to all in 2001. A flat trail skirts the bay and a sandy beach and is great for runners, strollers, and dog walking, as well as for people and landscape watching. Fort Point, a Civil War-era brick stronghold, lies directly beneath the southern end of the Golden Gate Bridge span, and visitors here get some of the most spectacular views. At the end of the route, give a high-five to the Hopper's Hands plaque on the fence at Fort Point. Everyone's got their own version of the ritual, some with fist bumps and others with multiple high-fives. Former Golden Gate Bridge ironworker Ken Hopper noticed that people used this fence as a touchpoint before turning around and asked the bridge's sign maker to create the sign.

1199 East Beach
(415) 561-7752
nps.gov/prsf, presidio.gov

TIP
A good midway break point, the Warming Hut has casual but healthy food and drinks, especially soup, coffee, tea, and hot chocolate to keep you warm.

TAKE A LONG WALK
ON THE CALIFORNIA COASTAL TRAIL

Hiking in San Francisco isn't relegated to picking a hill to climb or taking a stroll through Golden Gate Park. The California Coastal Trail is a 1,200-mile network of public trails that passes through fifteen California counties, and 10.5 miles of it run through San Francisco. The trail enters San Francisco from the south at Fort Funston. From there, the hike moves along Ocean Beach to the Cliff House, Lands End, and Lincoln Park, and then to China Beach before it enters the Presidio. The CCT passes along the rocky coastal bluffs with native blooms and shrubs and windswept Monterey cypress trees until it reaches the Golden Gate and Pacific Overlooks. The trail leads north to the Golden Gate Bridge, which is its last point in San Francisco, but it continues across the bridge and into the Marin Headlands on its long route through the state.

californiacoastaltrail.info

TIP
A short side trip (0.7 miles) from the California Coastal Trail in the Presidio, the Batteries to Bluffs Trail is worth the detour. The moderate-to-difficult trail snakes along the Presidio's wild western shoreline among native dune plants and wildflowers to Battery Crosby, a historic gun battery.

GET OUT OF TOWN
ON A DAY TRIP

San Francisco is the perfect home base for exploring more of California, and there are a number of easy day-trip options that will have you back in the city by nightfall. **Napa Valley**, just an hour from the Golden Gate Bridge, has more than four hundred wineries, scores of top-rated restaurants, and a wealth of outdoor adventures. **Sonoma Valley** has more than one hundred wineries, a historic California Mission, great restaurants, and miles of hiking and biking trails. The **Santa Cruz Beach Boardwalk** is full of roller coaster and arcade-game fun, but you can also head into the **Santa Cruz Mountains** to visit redwoods and wineries. **Half Moon Bay**—known for the big-wave surf spot, Mavericks—is also the World's Pumpkin Capital, and its fall harvest festival draws crowds from all over. Just across the Golden Gate Bridge, the **Marin Headlands** and **Mount Tamalpais** have some of the most beautiful hiking and biking trails in the Bay Area. While you're in the neighborhood, find serenity among the towering coastal redwoods of **Muir Woods National Monument**. **Point Reyes National Seashore** protects more than 1,500 plant species and eighty miles of shoreline, and the picture-perfect village of **Sausalito** is an ideal lunch spot just across the bay.

TIP
Within four hours of San Francisco,
you can also reach Yosemite, Lake Tahoe,
Big Sur, and many other treasures
of the Golden State.

PLAY ALL DAY
IN GOLDEN GATE PARK

Developed in the 1880s, Golden Gate Park is a lush green strip that covers more than one thousand acres from the center of the city to the far western edge. It's larger than New York's Central Park and is the fifth-most-visited city park in the United States. Top attractions include one of the largest museums of natural history in the world, the **California Academy of Sciences**. The copper-clad **de Young Museum** showcases collections of seventeenth- through twentieth-century American art, as well as art of the Pacific, Africa, and the Americas. Wedged between the two museums is the **Spreckels Temple of Music** (often referred to as the Bandshell) and Music Concourse, where free concerts sing out on summer Sundays. The **Japanese Tea Garden** is the oldest public Japanese garden in the United States. The oldest building in the park houses the **Conservatory of Flowers**, where rare and unusual plants are displayed and cultivated. The **San Francisco Botanical Garden** takes advantage of San Francisco's unique microclimate to recreate conditions of high-elevation tropical cloud forests around the world. Other beloved highlights include finding a quiet moment at the **National AIDS Memorial Grove**, visiting the majestic residents of the **Bison Paddock**, viewing the springtime blooms of the **Queen Wilhelmina Tulip Garden**, and taking classes at the **Sharon Art Studio**.

Bordered by Great Hwy., Fulton St., Lincoln Way, and Stanyan St.
goldengatepark.com

FUN FACT

The often-missed Garden of Shakespeare's Flowers in Golden Gate Park was created in 1927 and has flowers mentioned in the works of the famous bard.

SPEND A DAY
OUT ON THE BAY

Water views are nearly everywhere in San Francisco, and there are plenty of ways to get a closer look. The San Francisco Bay may not seem like a gigantic body of water while gazing across it, but when you're in a kayak or stand-up paddleboard (SUP), you feel appropriately small. Rent from **City Kayak** in South Beach and head for AT&T Park's McCovey Cove to catch home run "splash hits" from a Giants game. Take the family out for a calm brunch, lunch, or dinner cruise aboard one of **Hornblower's** dining yachts. Or, if adrenaline is more your taste, **ACsailingSF** takes guests out on the *USA 76*, an International America's Cup Class racing yacht. The Blue & Gold Fleet's *RocketBoat*—a highly maneuverable speedboat that makes quick, tight turns—may be the wildest ride on the bay. The **Blue & Gold Fleet** and the **Red & White Fleet** offer a variety of cruising adventures that help you see San Francisco Bay's greatest highlights. **Adventure Cat Sailing Charters** invites guests to experience the beauty of San Francisco from the deck of a spacious catamaran that cruises right under the Golden Gate Bridge.

TIP
Need calmer water? Head to Golden Gate Park's Stow Lake, where you can enjoy the slower pace and rent pedal boats, rowboats, and electric boats.

City Kayak
Pier 40
(888) 966-0953
citykayak.com

Hornblower
Embarcadero, Pier 3
(415) 788-8866
hornblower.com

ACsailingSF
Pier 39
(415) 990-9992
acsailingsf.com

Blue & Gold Fleet
Pier 41
(415) 705-8200
blueandgoldfleet.com

Red & White Fleet
Pier 43 ½
(415) 673-2900
redandwhite.com

Adventure Cat Sailing Charters
Pier 39
(415) 777-1630
adventurecat.com

EXPLORE
ON TWO WHEELS

Despite the hills, San Francisco has an enthusiastic cycling culture, and if you're keen to two-wheel it, the **San Francisco Bicycle Coalition** (SFBC) has a wealth of resources, from local bicycle laws and suggested routes and maps to the dos and don'ts of bringing your bike on public transportation. The Bay Area's bike-share program, **Ford GoBike**, has thousands of public bikes for use all over the Bay Area. Use their online station map to find the one closest to you, as well as a regularly updated report on how many bikes are available. There are also myriad bicycle rental outfitters (some of whom offer bike tours, as well), like **Blazing Saddles Bike Rentals and Tours**, **San Francisco Bicycle Rentals**, **Basically Free Bike Rentals**, and **The Bike Hut**.

FUN FACT
San Francisco's most famous bike route is the Wiggle, which stretches for a mile from Market Street to Golden Gate Park. Keep your eyes on the road, but don't miss the incredible murals along the way.

San Francisco Bicycle Coalition
1720 Market St.
(415) 431-2453
sfbike.org

Ford GoBike
(855) 480-2453
fordgobike.com

Blazing Saddles Bike Rentals and Tours
Seven locations throughout the city.
(415) 202-8888
blazingsaddles.com

San Francisco Bicycle Rentals
Shops at Fisherman's Wharf, Golden Gate Park,
and the Ferry Building.
(415) 922-4537
bikerentalsanfrancisco.com

Basically Free Bike Rentals
1196 Columbus St.
(628) 208-0402
basicallyfree.com

The Bike Hut
Pier 40
(415) 543-4335
thebikehut.org

CULTURE AND HISTORY

FOLLOW
THE BEAT GENERATION

The Beats were a collection of writers, artists, and thinkers who congregated in 1950s San Francisco. The North Beach neighborhood was the stomping grounds for artists Jack Kerouac, Allen Ginsburg, Gary Snyder, and other prominent poets and writers of the time. Duck into **The Beat Museum**, home to an extensive collection of Beat memorabilia. The museum also offers guided tours of its own collection, as well as North Beach walking tours for groups. A meeting place for the Beats, **City Lights Booksellers & Publishers** was co-founded by Beat poet Lawrence Ferlinghetti and was responsible for publishing Allen Ginsburg's infamous poem, "Howl." Walk through Jack Kerouac Alley to **Vesuvio Cafe**, a longtime favorite bar of the Beats. Across the street, Specs Twelve Adler Museum Cafe is a dive bar with a fascinating collection of curios. Another bar that was a favorite of the Beats is Tosca Cafe, the third-oldest bar in the city. Don't miss the house cappuccino, an espresso-free cocktail of steamed hot chocolate with brandy. Caffe Trieste was a choice writing spot for Beat figures, as well. Grab an Italian-style espresso at the first true espresso bar on the West Coast and find your own inspiration.

FUN FACT
Although he was not among the Beats, Francis Ford Coppola spent months at Caffe Trieste writing the screenplay for *The Godfather*.

The Beat Museum
540 Broadway
(800) 537-6822
kerouac.com

City Lights Booksellers & Publishers
261 Columbus Ave.
(415) 362-8193
citylights.com

Vesuvio Cafe
255 Columbus Ave.
(415) 362-3370
vesuvio.com

Specs Twelve Adler Museum Cafe
12 William Saroyan Place
(415) 421-4112

Tosca Cafe
242 Columbus Ave.
(415) 986-9651
toscacafesf.com

Caffe Trieste
601 Vallejo St.
(415) 392-6739
caffetrieste.com

ESCAPE
TO ALCATRAZ

The island of Alcatraz was reserved for military use in 1850, the same year California became a state. In the next decade, a fortress and the West Coast's first operational lighthouse were constructed. By the end of the 1850s, the U.S. Army had begun holding military prisoners there. In 1934, the Army facilities became a federal prison intended for housing a criminal population too difficult or dangerous to be handled by other U.S. penitentiaries. Over the years, until the penitentiary was closed in 1963, there were only fourteen escape attempts involving thirty-six inmates (only five of whom were never recovered). Alcatraz Cruises is the official ferry provider to Alcatraz and back to San Francisco. A variety of options are available, including a day tour, night tour, and behind-the-scenes tour. There is also a combined ticket to Alcatraz and Angel Island.

Alcatraz Island	Alcatraz Cruises
(415) 561-4900	Pier 33
nps.gov/alca	(415) 981-7625
	alcatrazcruises.com

TIP
For more than a century, gardens were an important part of everyday life for the island's officers, families, and prisoners. These historic gardens not only illustrate the importance of gardening to the human spirit, but also the ecological benefits of sustainable gardening.

SLEUTH
WITH DASHIELL HAMMET AND SAM SPADE

Although Dashiell Hammett lived in San Francisco for less than a decade, his association with the city remains strong. *The Maltese Falcon*, the best known of his novels, is set in San Francisco, and you can follow main character Sam Spade around the city. One of the best sources for separating noir fact from hard-boiled fiction is Don Herron, who has led The Dashiell Hammett Tour in San Francisco since 1977. In a trench coat and snap-brim hat, he leads inquisitive literary fans through the streets that Sam Spade stalked, as well as highlights that figure in Dashiell Hammett's history. Perched in John's Grill is a replica of the Maltese Falcon made famous by the novel and the 1941 film noir classic. On Burritt Street near the intersection of Stockton and Bush Streets is a plaque that marks the place where Miles Archer, Sam Spade's partner in *The Maltese Falcon*, is shot and killed by the book's femme fatale, Brigid O'Shaughnessy.

The Dashiell Hammett Tour
donherron.com/the-tour

John's Grill
63 Ellis St., (415) 986-0069
johnsgrill.com

FUN FACT
Hammett's first job in San Francisco was for the Pinkerton National Detective Agency, which was housed at the time in the Flood Building at 870 Market St.

FOLLOW THE BRONZE MEDALLIONS
ALONG THE BARBARY COAST TRAIL

Transformed overnight by the California Gold Rush of 1849, San Francisco became a bustling tent city. The colorful port area of saloons, brothels, gambling halls, and lodging houses was known during this wild time as the Barbary Coast. Today's Barbary Coast Trail revisits this chapter in the city's history and tracks San Francisco's growth over the past two hundred years. A project of the San Francisco Museum and Historical Society, the 3.7-mile walking trail is speckled with historical landmarks, lively pubs and cafés, and museums, all connected by approximately 180 bronze medallions imbedded into the city sidewalks. A map and official trail guide is available at visitor centers, local bookstores, and online (there are also downloadable audio tours).

57 Post St., Ste. 614
(415) 454-2355
barbarycoasttrail.org

FUN FACT
On Commercial Street, between Montgomery and Kearny Streets, is a small green space that marks the location of Emperor Norton's Imperial Palace.

LET THE RAINBOW FLAG FLY
AT PRIDE

The annual weekend-long San Francisco Pride Celebration, which takes place on the last full weekend in June, is a celebration of diversity that draws people from all over the world to descend on the downtown parade and festival, making it the largest LGTBQ celebration in the country. Spontaneous revelry rules, costumes are more than welcome, and it's a chance to reflect on history, both happy and sad. The festivities begin on Saturday in Civic Center Plaza, where the main stage features music and competitions, and encompass more than twenty community-run stages and more than three hundred exhibitors. Sunday's parade is the highlight of the weekend, with more than two hundred parade contingents marching along Market Street through the heart of the city, delighting more than one hundred thousand spectators. Every color of the rainbow is present—from fabulous strutters to a huge range of causes to the loud and proud Dykes on Bikes motorcycle group.

Parade route: From Market St. at Beale St. (Financial District)
to Market at 8th St. (Civic Center)
Celebration: Civic Center
sfpride.org

TIP
Indulgent celebration is embraced on this weekend, so be kind to your future self and pack plenty of water and sunscreen (even if it's foggy out).

FIND CULTURE
IN SAN FRANCISCO MUSEUMS

Some of the United States' most diverse art collections, paired with interactive science exhibits and educational programs, make San Francisco museums not only worth visiting, but also worthy of a top-place spot on a traveler's itinerary.

TIP
While it's ideal to support these museums with your admission dollars, several of them offer free admission days, listed on each museum's website.

San Francisco Museum of Modern Art, the first museum on the West Coast devoted solely to modern and contemporary art, opened in 1935.
151 3rd St., (415) 357-4000, sfmoma.org

de Young Museum is renowned for its American art, textile art, and art from Africa, Oceania, and the Americas.
50 Hagiwara Tea Garden Dr., (415) 750-3600, deyoung.famsf.org

California Academy of Sciences is an aquarium, planetarium, and natural history museum, all under one living roof.
55 Music Concourse Dr., (415) 379-8000, calacademy.org

Legion of Honor has an art collection that spans four thousand years of ancient and European art and houses the Achenbach Foundation for Graphic Arts.
100 34th Ave., (415) 750-3600, legionofhonor.famsf.org

Asian Art Museum is home to one of the world's most diverse collections of art and objects—spanning six thousand years—from the Asian continent.
200 Larkin St., (415) 581-3500, asianart.org

Exploratorium isn't just for kids. This interactive museum inspires creativity and curiosity, something we all need.
Embarcadero, Pier 15, (415) 528-4444 , exploratorium.edu

Museum of African Diaspora celebrates the art, history, and culture resulting from the migration of Africans throughout the world.
685 Mission St., (415) 358-7200, moadsf.org

Contemporary Jewish Museum presents innovative exhibitions and educational programs on Jewish culture and history.
736 Mission St., (415) 655-7800, thecjm.org

APPRECIATE MURAL ART
IN THE MISSION DISTRICT

San Francisco has hundreds of murals scattered throughout the cityscape; however, the largest concentration is in the Mission District, and they are among the best ways to see the neighborhood's cultural heritage. For the easiest way to see the best of the artwork, sign up for one of the several different guided mural walks offered by Precita Eyes Mural Arts & Visitor Center every weekend. Tours are conducted by muralists, so you're bound to get the straight story. The community-based nonprofit also shows works by local artists. If you'd rather do a self-tour, some don't-miss spots in the Mission are: Balmy Alley, Clarion Alley, the *Carnaval* mural at 24th Street and South Van Ness (showing San Francisco's first Carnaval event in 1979), and the *Maestrapeace* Mural on the Women's Building at 1343 18th Street (this mural was painted in 1994 by a who's who of Bay Area muralists).

2981 24th St.
(415) 285-2287
precitaeyes.org

TIP
Drop by Precita Eyes Mural Arts & Visitor Center for a map that will help guide your mural adventure.

GET IMMERSED
IN ANDY GOLDSWORTHY'S OUTDOOR ART

Best known for his work with natural materials, Andy Goldsworthy is a contemporary artist whose work heightens the viewer's awareness of the fine line between nature and art. San Francisco is home to five of his works. *Drawn Stone* (2005) appears as a continuous, seemingly random crack that runs north from the edge of Golden Gate Park's Music Concourse roadway into the courtyard of the de Young Museum. In the Presidio, Goldsworthy has four site-specific installations that celebrate the Presidio's landmark forest in an organically evolving project. *Spire* (2008) is a one-hundred-foot-tall tapering peak created from fastening together thirty-seven Monterey cypress trunks. *Wood Line* (2011) is a curvy 1,200-foot line of branches tucked into the forest floor. *Tree Fall* (2013) was constructed by combining local clay with a tree. *Earth Wall* (2014) is located inside the Presidio Officers' Club.

de Young Museum
50 Hagiwara Tea Garden Dr.
(415) 750-3600
deyoung.famsf.org

Presidio Visitor Center
210 Lincoln Blvd.
(415) 561-4323
nps.gov/prsf, presidio.gov

TIP
Each of the Goldsworthy installations in the Presidio can be visited individually or together via a three-mile hiking loop along the Presidio's trails. A Goldsworthy-specific map is available through the Presidio Trust.

SNAP A PHOTO
AT THE PALACE OF FINE ARTS

At the eastern edge of the Presidio stands a tranquil urban temple that's become a San Francisco treasure. The Palace of Fine Arts was originally built for the 1915 Panama–Pacific International Exposition—an event to celebrate the rise of the city from the destruction of the 1906 earthquake and fire, as well as the completion of the Panama Canal. The palace, created with plaster and burlap fiber by Bernard Maybeck, emulated a Roman ruin reflected in a pool. It was supposed to be torn down with all the other buildings, but it was too beloved to destroy. By the late 1940s and early 1950s, the temporary building was beginning to crumble. A combination of funding was collected, and the original Palace of Fine Arts was demolished in 1964—but only to rebuild it using more permanent materials. The reborn palace opened in 1967. Today, it's one of the most-photographed sites in the city, as well as a popular wedding location, performance venue, and linger-in-the-sun spot.

3601 Lyon St.
(415) 608-2220
palaceoffinearts.com

FUN FACT
Maybeck's masterpiece was the mirror of a ruin that existed not for its own sake, but to show "the mortality of grandeur and the vanity of human wishes."

PICTURE PRETTY PAINTED LADIES

The picturesque Painted Ladies on Steiner Street at Alamo Square have been around for a long time. They were constructed between 1892 and 1896—just seven of forty-eight thousand San Francisco houses built in the Victorian and Edwardian styles between 1849 and 1915. After all the new money of the Gold Rush came flooding in, grand houses were built that leaned towards the flashy Queen Anne style, with multiple balconies, large porches, bay windows, turrets, and decorated rooflines. All the ladies are single-family homes and aren't open for tours. This tight, escalating formation of Victorian homes is also called Postcard Row, and the view of them in front of a backdrop of downtown skyscrapers provides a stunning contrast for many visiting the city.

710–720 Steiner St.

FUN FACT

Sure, the Tanner family from *Full House* picnicked in Alamo Square Park, with a view of Postcard Row and the Painted Ladies, but the building that's pictured in the opening credits as their home is at 1709 Broderick Street.

VIEW THE CITY
FROM ATOP COIT TOWER

The fluted tower atop Telegraph Hill stands thanks to Lillie Hitchcock Coit, a San Francisco eccentric who smoked cigars and wore men's clothing to gain entrance to gamble in North Beach's men-only storefronts. She was considered the "mascot" firefighter of Knickerbocker Engine Company No. 5. When she died in 1929, she gave one-third of her estate to the city. The 210-foot Coit Tower, made of unpainted concrete, was designed by architect Arthur Brown Jr. and completed in 1933. Don't believe the romantic story—it wasn't built to look like a fire hose nozzle. The tower murals depict life in California during the Great Depression and were created by artists employed under the Public Works of Art Project, a precursor to the Works Progress Administration (WPA). Take an elevator up to Coit Tower's observation deck for spectacular views of San Francisco, the bay, and the Golden Gate and Bay Bridges.

1 Telegraph Hill Blvd.
(415) 249-0995
sfrecpark.org

TIP
Avoid the elevator line at Coit Tower by purchasing a time-specific ticket. Docent-led mural tour tickets are available in advance, as well.

CELEBRATE CHINESE NEW YEAR
IN CHINATOWN

As old as the city of San Francisco, Chinatown is the second-largest Asian community in North America, and when Chinese New Year comes around on the calendar, there's no better place to be in the city. The New Year celebration is a festive month of events that include the Chinese New Year Flower Fair, the Southwest Airlines Chinese New Year Parade, and many more. Flowers symbolize the start of the festivities, and shoppers can buy flowers, oranges, and good-luck items from the colorful booths on Grant Avenue. The biggest event of Chinese New Year is the nighttime illuminated parade, with elaborate floats, marching bands, and a Golden Dragon (288 feet long and powered by a team of more than 180 people). On parade weekend, there's also a two-day Chinese Community Street Fair on Grant Avenue, with traditional and modern entertainment from folk dancing to acrobats and lion dancing to Chinese cultural arts.

Parade route: 2nd St. and Market St. to Columbus Ave. chineseparade.com

TIP
Dress warmly and bring an umbrella if attending the parade because it happens rain or shine. Stay until the end to see the Golden Dragon—a crowd favorite.

DISCOVER SAN FRANCISCO'S OLDEST ARCHITECTURE
AT MISSION DOLORES

The modest adobe structure in San Francisco's Mission District is the city's oldest building. Built in 1776, Misión San Francisco de Asís was named after Saint Francis of Assisi, the founder of the Franciscan order. But everyone knows it as Mission Dolores, nicknamed for its nearby creek, Arroyo de Nuestra Señora de los Dolores (the Creek of Our Lady of Sorrows). In the mission's cemetery, an estimated five thousand people have been laid to rest since 1830, including Ohlone and Miwok settlers and notable residents of the city's early days. The mission gardens contain the same types of plants as they did during the eighteenth century. An Ohlone ethno-botanic garden shows examples of Native American plants and artifacts, and the rose garden was a gift of the Golden Gate Rose Society—tended by members every week.

3321 16th St.
(415) 621-8203
missiondolores.org

FUN FACT

A hidden mural behind the wooden altar in the sanctuary was painted by native peoples in the late eighteenth century but has been covered by a reredos, a baroque-style relief sculpture, since 1796. The mural was digitized in 2000 to allow visitors to get a look at it.

STROLL AMONG THE RUINS
OF SUTRO BATHS

Looking at them from the hillside near the Cliff House restaurant, it is difficult to imagine that the low concrete walls and twisted steel supports that skirt the edge of the ocean were once part of a massive glass-enclosed structure that housed public baths. Adolph Sutro's giant center for recreation and entertainment opened in 1896 and spread over three acres. The structure included seven pools heated to various temperatures, slides, diving boards, restaurants, a museum, coin-operated games, more than five hundred dressing rooms, and seating for 3,700 spectators. At first, the baths were enormously popular, but over time the costs of maintaining the building became a burden. The structure was destined for demolition in the mid-1960s so that high-rise condominiums could be built, but it caught fire before any of that could happen. The ruins are publicly accessible and the main paths are easy to traverse. Use caution when walking among them because the terrain is rough and can be dangerous in bad weather.

680 Point Lobos Ave.

(415) 426-5240, nps.gov/goga

TIP
The best time of day for taking a good photo of Sutro Baths is at sunset on a weekday—when fewer visitors are present.

VISIT THE PEOPLE'S PALACE:
SAN FRANCISCO'S CITY HALL

The city hall you see in San Francisco today isn't the first. It was built of steel, granite, and white marble to replace Old City Hall, which was destroyed in the 1906 earthquake and fire. San Francisco's new City Hall was built over two years, to open in time for the beginning of the 1915 Panama–Pacific International Exposition. Designed by Arthur Brown Jr., the same architect who designed Coit Tower, the Beaux-Arts building's sweeping grand staircase, gilt detailing, and majestic dome (that's forty-two feet taller than that of the nation's capitol) continue to awe visitors and residents alike. Docent-led tours (that last from forty-five minutes to an hour) are available on weekdays at 10:00 a.m., 12:00 p.m., and 2:00 p.m. Sign up at the Docent Tour kiosk, near the Goodlett Place lobby next to the elevators.

1 Dr. Carlton B. Goodlett Pl.
(415) 554-4000
sfgov.org/cityhall

TIP
Each evening at sunset, more than 220 LED lighting fixtures illuminate City Hall's exterior. On special occasions, the usual soft white glow is replaced by colors to celebrate events, seasons, and holidays.

RELIVE SAN FRANCISCO HISTORY
ON FOOT

In the old TV show, the streets of San Francisco were made for epic high-speed car chases, but in real life, walking is more the norm. Step into one of these walking tours that offer special insight into food, local history, culture, and other curiosities that make this such a fascinating city.

TIP
Book ahead. Most tours are capped at a maximum number of people.

HOOF IT

Secret Food Tours
Zeros in on the city's vibrant Mission District
and its local history.
(628) 246-0095, secretfoodtours.com

Wild SF Walking Tours
Haunted spots, radical history, the era of free love,
and other funky tours.
(415) 580-1849, wildsftours.com

San Francisco Food Tour
Nibble through the alleyways and history of Chinatown.
(888) 358-8687, sffoodtour.com

Emperor Norton's Fantastic San Francisco Time Machine
Follow in the footsteps of Emperor Norton I, self-proclaimed
Emperor of the United States and Protector of Mexico.
(415) 644-8513, emperornortontour.com

Free Tours by Foot
The Secrets, Scandals, and Scoundrels tour spotlights
the dark side of San Francisco's history.
(415) 295-2207, freetoursbyfoot.com

Avital Tours
The Italian-centric North Beach neighborhood tour offers
four courses at four different restaurants.
(415) 355-4044, avitaltours.com

Discovery Street Tours
Investigate the science of everyday life, from seismic forces that
shaped the city to San Francisco stories of innovation.
(415) 663-6768, discoverystreettours.com

DISCOVER SEAFARING HISTORY
AT SAN FRANCISCO MARITIME NATIONAL HISTORICAL PARK

Ships played crucial roles in San Francisco's history—from Spanish settlement to Gold Rush hopefuls, from those loaded with building and farming equipment to those armed for World Wars I and II. But with each passing year, more and more of San Francisco Bay's historic vessels became obsolete. The San Francisco Maritime National Historical Park maintains and exhibits the largest collection of historic ships in the United States, four of which are open to visitors: *Balclutha* (1886), *Eureka* (1890), *C. A. Thayer* (1895), and *Hercules* (1907). There's also a visitor center, a museum in the Aquatic Park Bathhouse Building, and the largest maritime library west of the Mississippi. Park ranger-led interpretive programs and demonstrations are held on the historic ships and the Hyde Street Pier, where they're moored.

499 Jefferson St.
(415) 561-7000, nps.gov/safr, maritime.org

TIP
Alma, a sixty-foot wooden-hulled scow schooner built in 1891, is the last of her kind, and she still sails from June through November. Make reservations at (415) 447-5000.

MAKE A STOP
AT LOTTA'S FOUNTAIN

In the hustle and bustle of San Francisco's Financial District, you might miss the city's oldest surviving monument: Lotta's Fountain. On the corner of Market, Geary, and Kearny Streets, the cast-iron sculpture is painted bronze and adorned with griffins, lions' heads, and other ornaments. The fountain was cast in Philadelphia, shipped to San Francisco around Cape Horn, and reassembled and presented in 1875 to the citizens of San Francisco by Lotta Crabtree, one of the most famous entertainers of her day. After the 1906 earthquake, the fountain, which was one of the few remaining structures downtown, became a meeting point for many people trying to reassemble their families. In the years since, the city has held a ceremony here every April 18 at 5:12 a.m., the moment of the main shock, that is attended by earthquake survivors and dignitaries.

Corner of Market, Geary, and Kearny Sts.

FUN FACT
Even though the last known survivor of the 1906 San Francisco earthquake and fire died in 2016, April 18 earthquake remembrance ceremonies continue at Lotta's Fountain.

MEET THE NEIGHBORS
AT A LIVELY STREET FAIR

The summer season brings San Franciscans outside to celebrate the city's diverse neighborhoods and denizens. The wealth of street fairs and festivals ranges from very family friendly to decidedly no kids, unless you want to answer a barrage of questions.

TIP
There are even more summer fairs, plus festivals occurring throughout the year. Check the San Francisco Travel Association events calendar. sftravel.com

Union Street Music Festival

Includes more than twenty-four live bands covering four different genres (jazz, blues, country, bluegrass) scattered across five blocks.
Gough St. to Fillmore St., unionstreetfestival.com

Juneteenth SF

One of the largest African American celebrations in California, Juneteenth celebrates historical awareness and strengthens the community. Call for parade route.
(510) 692-2514, sfjuneteenth.com

North Beach Festival

San Francisco's oldest street fair includes the animal blessing at the National Shrine of Saint Francis.
(800) 310-6563, northbeachbusinessassociation.com

Haight-Ashbury Street Fair

Connects Golden Gate Park with the famed Haight-Ashbury corner for a day of summer fun.
Between Haight St. and Ashbury St., haightashburystreetfair.org

Fillmore Jazz Festival

Blends art and soul into the largest free jazz festival on the West Coast. Takes place over Independence Day weekend.
Fillmore St. between Jackson St. and Eddy St.
fillmorejazzfestival.com

Nihonmachi Street Fair

Brings together Asian-Pacific American life with San Francisco culture in Japantown.
Post St. between Laguna St. and Fillmore St.
nihonmachistreetfair.org

Folsom Street Fair

Embraces leather and fetish, and it's the ideal time to leave the kids with a babysitter elsewhere.
Folsom St. from 8th St. to 13th St., folsomstreetfair.com

Castro Street Fair

Founded by Harvey Milk, celebrates the diversity of the neighborhood with live entertainment and local artists. Usually held the first Sunday of October.
Castro St. at Market St., castrostreetfair.org

HELP ARTISTS THRIVE
AT THE MINNESOTA STREET PROJECT

San Francisco's Union Square has long been the heart of the city's commercial gallery district. In recent years, however, artists and art dealers have been priced out of their traditional haunts. The Minnesota Street Project, which opened in 2016 in three former warehouses and industrial workshops, is home to a gallery space for art dealers, studio space for local artists, and an art storage facility. The restaurant, Alta, is a joint project between Chef Daniel Patterson and the Minnesota Street Project and is a vibrant part of the art community and the neighborhood at large. The galleries on Minnesota Street and on 25th Street are open to the public, although the artist studio on Minnesota Street is not. Each gallery has individual hours, so check the Minnesota Street Project site in advance before visiting.

1275 Minnesota St. and 1150 25th St.
(415) 243-0825
minnesotastreetproject.com

TIP
Stop in at the Minnesota Street Project store before you leave. The proceeds are split between participating artists and the project, and the project's portion is used to further reduce the rents charged to resident artists.

CLIMB HALFWAY TO THE STARS
ON CABLE CARS

Once upon a time, cable car lines served the entire city of San Francisco, and before the 1906 earthquake and fire, there were more than six hundred cable cars in operation. Designated a National Historic Landmark, they've left their mark on the city in many ways. Cable car inventor Andrew Smith Halladie tested the first car on Clay Street in 1873, and within sixteen years there were eight cable car companies and fifty-three miles of track in the city. Today, three cable car lines remain, run by the San Francisco Municipal Transportation Agency (SFMTA): Powell/Hyde, Powell/Mason, and California Street. Although many people find it easiest to catch the cable car at the main turnaround (Powell line cars) or the end stop (California line cars), you are allowed to get on the car at any stop along the route.

sfmta.com

TIP
For more on the history of San Francisco cable cars, visit the Cable Car Museum, where you can still see the churning cables that pull the cars across the city.
(1201 Mason St., (415) 474-1887, cablecarmuseum.org)

SHOPPING AND FASHION

SUPPORT GOLDEN GATE NATIONAL PARK
AT THE WARMING HUT

The two-story wood-frame "hut" on the Crissy Field waterfront path near the foot of the Golden Gate Bridge was built in 1909 as a U.S. Engineer Storehouse. Known as the Warming Hut now, it's a great place to rest after a run, meet friends for coffee, snap the ultimate bridge photo, and pick up a San Francisco souvenir. Besides being a café, the Warming Hut is also a park information center and a gift shop with city-themed cards, artwork, clothing, locally made gift items, and books. Best of all, proceeds benefit the Golden Gate National Parks Conservancy's mission to preserve its parklands for future generations to enjoy.

983 Marine Dr.
(415) 561-3040
parksconservancy.org

TIP
If you're looking for a place to plug-in, sorry—the Warming Hut does not have Wi-Fi. Enjoy the view instead!

TREASURE HUNT
AT TREASUREFEST

Since its 2011 debut, TreasureFest (formerly known as Treasure Island Flea) has lured flea market fans to Treasure Island, a former naval station sitting on a man-made patch of land in the bay. The flea market started as a place for indie designers and artists to show off their goods, but it has morphed into a two-day event that is Northern California's largest monthly festival. Shop more than four hundred vendors for upcycled goods, jewelry, local art, one-of-a-kind new and vintage clothing, antiques, and myriad other finds. When you get hungry, a lineup of the Bay Area's best food trucks is on standby. TreasureFest is held year-round, rain or shine, on the last Saturday and Sunday of each month from 10 a.m. to 4 p.m. Entry is five dollars, and kids under twelve are free.

Pier 1, Treasure Island
(415) 898-0245
treasurefest.com

TIP
Learn all about the island's history at the Treasure Island Museum, located in the Art Moderne Building One.

TEST YOUR
CREDIT CARD'S METTLE
AT UNION SQUARE

Described literally, Union Square is a 2.6-acre public plaza boxed in by Geary, Post, Powell, and Stockton Streets in downtown San Francisco, but when you say "Union Square" to locals, one word comes to mind—shopping! World-renowned brand names and haute couture labels cluster around Union Square and for several blocks in every direction, happily taunting the limits of your platinum card. You'll also find hotels, bars, restaurants, and theaters in the neighborhood, making it a one-stop entertainment district. The multipurpose plaza is also home to year-round civic events and celebrations and is especially lovely during the holidays when an ice rink, menorah, and Christmas tree are set up, kicking off the festive season.

visitunionsquaresf.com

FUN FACT
Pedestrian-only Maiden Lane, just off Union Square, now showcases top luxury shops, but in bawdier times it was the city's red-light district.

BAG ONE-OF-A-KIND FINDS
ON VALENCIA STREET

An indie spirit reigns on this pulsating artery in the Mission District. Lined with scores of eclectic and vintage clothing stores and specialty boutiques, Valencia Street will keep you shopping for hours.

Shopping list

Mel Rice Ceramica
A closet-sized nook of wooden shelves stacked with hand-thrown bowls, mugs, vases, and more.
853 Valencia St., (415) 941-7975
melriceceramica.com

Serendipity
Fun and whimsical greeting cards and locally sourced gift items and artwork.
803 Valencia St., (415) 401-8760
serendipitysanfrancisco.com

The Pirate Store
Arg! Grab your eye patch, pirate garb, hooks, or captain's quill, all benefiting a nonprofit writing and tutoring center.
826 Valencia St., (415) 642-5905
826valencia.org

Needles and Pens
Art gallery and emporium showcasing international and locally made books, self-published zines, and handmade goods.
1173 Valencia St., (415) 872-9189
needles-pens.com

Wallflower
An ever-changing vintage selection of clothing, home decor, and accessories.
1176 Valencia St.
(415) 341-0314
shopwallflower.com

DECK YOUR WALLS
WITH SAN FRANCISCO ART
AT SF OPEN STUDIOS

SF Open Studios is the largest and longest-running open studios program in the United States. Produced by ArtSpan, the month-long event began in 1975 with just twenty artists. Fast-forward to today, and the citywide art extravaganza spans four weekends in October and November and invites art lovers to meet more than eight hundred participating artists in various neighborhoods across the city. For art collectors or just curious consumers, this means one-of-a kind pieces and an insight into a vibrant, world-class artistic community that celebrates the creative and diverse energy at the core of this city. Best of all, SF Open Studios is free and open to the public.

(415) 861-9838
artspan.org

TIP
ArtSpan Open Studios has an app you can download.

FILL UP YOUR BAGS
ON FILLMORE STREET

Located between the neighborhoods of Japantown and Pacific Heights, this retail and entertainment stretch between Jackson and Geary has everything from upscale fashion brands to one-off boutiques and a slew of cafés and restaurants to fuel a shop-til-you-drop day.

Kiehl's
A beauty chain with skincare, hair, and beauty products for men and women.
1971 Fillmore St.
(415) 359-9260
kiehls.com

Intermix
NYC-born chain of upscale women's clothing stores with a selection of trendy shoes and accessories.
2223 Fillmore St.
(415) 315-0200
intermixonline.com

Heidi Says
A must on Fillmore since 2000, with a wide selection of clothing from established and new designers.
2426 Fillmore St.
(415) 749-0655
heidisays.com

Frye
The 153-year-old boot and leather goods maker's nine-hundred-square-foot store carries leather footwear, bags, and accessories.
2047 Fillmore St.
(415) 346-3793
thefryecompany.com

Nest
For a home that's as colorful and trendy as you are, look no further.
2300 Fillmore St.
(415) 292-6199
nestsf.com

READ UP
AT AN INDEPENDENT BOOKSTORE

Bookstores may be a thing of the past in some cities, but San Francisco's independent booksellers are still cherished.

FUN FACT
Launched in California in 2014, Independent Bookstore Day (the last Saturday in April) has since gone national.

BOOK LIST

Green Apple Books
From its small beginnings in 1967 to eight
thousand square feet of used and new titles.
506 Clement St., (415) 387-2272, greenapplebooks.com

City Lights Bookstore
A landmark bookseller of alternative
culture titles, founded in 1953.
261 Columbus Ave., (415) 362-8193, citylights.com

Dog Eared Books
Read, sniff, and thumb through new and
used books at this Mission spot.
900 Valencia St., (415) 282-1901, dogearedbooks.com

Borderlands Books
For new and used mystery, sci-fi, horror,
and fantasy reads, the book stops here.
866 Valencia St., (415) 824-8203, borderlands-books.com

Book Passage
Big-name authors flock to this lively bookstore with
locations in Marin County and at the Ferry Building.
Market St. and the Embarcadero, (415) 835-1020
bookpassage.com

Books, Inc.
The West's oldest independent bookseller,
with locations around the Bay Area.
2251 Chestnut St., (415) 931-3633, booksinc.net

The Booksmith
Vibrant Haight-Ashbury literary hotspot with
a full roster of not-to-miss speakers.
1644 Haight St., (415) 863-8688, booksmith.com

STAY ON TREND
IN HAYES VALLEY

When the Central Freeway was destroyed in the 1989 Loma Prieta earthquake, the neighborhood of Hayes Valley emerged from its shadow and grew into a trendy and walkable neighborhood, chock-a-block with chic boutiques, coffee shops, bars, and some outstanding restaurants and cafés.

TIP
Take a break at the outdoor Biergarten at Hayes and Octavia Streets.

HAYES VALLEY BROWSING GUIDE

Lavish
Featuring women's clothes and accessories
along with books, gifts, and stationery.
549 Hayes St.
(415) 565-0540
shoplavish.com

Acoté
Contemporary French clothing brand that chose
San Francisco as its first U.S. address.
597 Hayes St.
(415) 525-4626
acoté.com

Undefeated
Stylish kicks for the shoe fetish crowd.
516 Hayes St.
(415) 437-2800
undefeated.com

Metier
Handcrafted statement jewelry and vintage finds.
546 Laguna St.
(415) 590-2998
metiersf.com

EI Home
Unique candles, bath and body products, and gifts.
348 Hayes St.
(415) 834-5456
eihomesf.com

MEET YOUR INNER HIPPIE
ON HAIGHT STREET

The Haight-Ashbury neighborhood is world-renowned for its summer-of-love history and still proudly clings to its hippie identity, which makes its main drag the perfect place to pick up groovy threads and souvenirs with an only-in-San Francisco vibe.

Gypsy Streetwear
Funky and eclectic is what this men's and women's clothing store prides itself on.
1399 Haight St.
(415) 513-5919

Wasteland
Handpicked designer and vintage alongside new indie finds.
1660 Haight St.
(415) 863-3150
shopwasteland.com

Amoeba Records
Vinyl lovers will go crazy at this landmark record store full of new and used tunes.
1855 Haight St.
(415) 831-1200
amoeba.com

Love on Haight
Tie-dye hats, sunglasses, clothing, and lots more.
1400 Haight St.
(415) 817-1027
loveonhaight-sf.com

Held Over
Secondhand retro and vintage goods and clothing since 1978.
1543 Haight St.
(415) 864-0818

TIP
Snap a photo in front of 710 Ashbury Street, a Queen Anne-style home where the Grateful Dead lived between 1966 and 1968.

SUGGESTED
ITINERARIES

FREE ACTIVITIES

Listen to Great Bands at a Music Festival, 40

Snap a Photo at the Palace of Fine Arts, 106

Bark with the Sea Lions at K-Dock, 69

Take In the View from Twin Peaks, 70

Choose Your Adventure at a San Francisco Beach, 76

People Watch like a San Franciscan at Mission Dolores Park, 82

Walk or Run from Crissy Field to Fort Point, 84

Make a Stop at Lotta's Fountain, 117

Take a Long Walk on the California Coastal Trail, 85

Appreciate Mural Art in the Mission District, 104

To Be or Not to Be at Shakespeare in the Park, 57

Get Immersed in Andy Goldsworthy's Outdoor Art, 105

Picture Pretty Painted Ladies, 107

Get a Mental Tune-Up at the Wave Organ, 59

Stroll among the Ruins of Sutro Baths, 112

Climb the Stairways to Heaven, 83

Meet the Neighbors at a Lively Fair, 118

Deck Your Walls With San Francisco Art at SF Open Studios, 128

Play All Day in Golden Gate Park, 88

FAMILY FUN

Get Up Close to Aquatic Life at the Aquarium of the Bay, 44

Get Your Mind Blown at the Marrakech Magic Theater, 51

ICONIC SAN FRANCISCO

ACTIVITIES
BY SEASON

The best weather advice about San Francisco is that you can always rely on the climate to change, sometimes by the hour, and differing from one part of the city to the next. That said, San Francisco enjoys a moderate Mediterranean climate, making it seem like an eternal spring. Fog can tend to be heavier in summer, while spring and fall can often be warmer. Since temperatures beside the Golden Gate average 54-65 degrees Fahrenheit in summer, and 48-56 degrees Fahrenheit in winter, outdoor activities can be enjoyed year-round.

WINTER

SPRING

INDEX